DIALYSIS: A MEMOIR

Lisa Frieden

For Kurt — Without him, I wouldn't be here.

All names except those of my immediate family have been changed out of respect for privacy.

Copyright © 2015 Lisa Frieden
Cover photo by Robert H. Russell

ISBN: 978-0-9969409-0-0

All rights reserved. No part of this book may be used or reproduced in any manner whatsoever without written permission, except in the case of brief quotations in critical articles and reviews. For information, please visit www.friedenpress.com.

Contents

Note to Reader
Chapter 1 - Before and After
Chapter 2 - Kidney Failure
Chapter 3 - Hemodialysis
Chapter 4 - Work
Chapter 5 - Meditation
Chapter 6 - Murphy's Law
Chapter 7 - PD Life
Chapter 8 - On the Road
Chapter 9 - Wait
Chapter 10 - Transplant
Chapter 11 - Back to Life
Chapter 12 - Denouement
Afterword
Acknowledgements
About the Author
Other Books by Lisa Frieden

Note to Reader

Kidney disease affects more than 26 million Americans, about one in nine adults, according to the National Kidney Foundation in 2014. More than 500,000 currently have end stage renal disease (ESRD)—permanent kidney failure.

These numbers are too big, too vast, too horrible for me to imagine. Even when I limit myself to my own experience, I still find ESRD exceeds my ability to make sense of it. This book is my attempt to come to terms with my experience, which was greatly influenced by its historical context during the dot com era of the late nineties in the San Francisco Bay Area.

I'm not comfortable uttering "universal truths" about illness or otherwise, and I can't speak for other people about their experiences. What I can do is share my story with you, what I went through, and how I discovered that while enduring great loss, I also gained new life, even if it was not the life I had originally planned.

For those of you who have had kidney failure or know someone who has, or for those of you considering donating a kidney, I hope you find this book helpful and perhaps a small beacon of light.

Chapter 1 - Before and After

The Crisis

December 14, 1998, began the same way most Mondays had the last couple of months. At 6:30 a.m., the alarm went off. I couldn't move. My husband Kurt didn't seem inclined to, either. We huddled under the blankets until 7 a.m. Then he got up to make breakfast. A massive weight seemed to press my body into the bed. Any exertion felt impossible. I couldn't move yet, at least not for a few more minutes. Sweat drenched my armpits as I shivered under the flannel sheets and down comforter. The clock ticked. It was almost 7:10 a.m. My client's press release would go out over the wire in five minutes, and there would be press follow-up to do. I had to get up and get the day started. So, I did.

Not hungry, I went through the motions of breakfast with Kurt, and then we mounted our bicycles and rode together through the chilly December morning. We parted at the corner of Hopkins and Peralta. He headed to the North Berkeley BART station, where he'd catch the subway into San Francisco and his Internet startup. I headed west toward Fourth Street and the bike route to Emeryville, where my boutique high tech PR firm was located.

I rode the bike path through Berkeley Aquatic Park, but I didn't register the crisp, clear skies over the San Francisco Bay or the Canadian geese waddling about on the grass. My legs were cramping underneath the black denim of my pants and my hands were going numb in the thin liner gloves as I gripped the handlebars. I ignored the rancid taste flooding my mouth. Instead, I focused on the day ahead and how much I had to do.

I made it to the office twenty minutes later, by 8:30 a.m., but then promptly rushed out again to buy Cara, my manager, a cup of coffee, payment for her having taken a 7 a.m. conference call for me. She was in the middle of a huge product launch for one of her East Coast startups, so she'd had to be at the office early, anyway.

I walked to the cafe through the bright morning and tried to ignore my body and the symptoms that had wracked it for the past month, that strange sensation of feeling chilled yet sweaty at the same time. I still had fifty follow-up emails to send out about my client's press release, so I hurried back with the coffee and got to work. At 9:10 a.m., my doctor phoned.

"Lisa, you've got to get yourself to the hospital. The lab results are back and—" She cleared her throat, as if she had something terrible to say but couldn't find the right words.

My heart began to race with a sense of dread and I hurried to close the office door. I sank into the chair and clutched the phone to my ear. "What is it?" I asked. Doctors don't usually call about routine lab results.

"They show something is wrong with your kidneys."

"My kidneys?"

I flashed back over my appointment with her last Friday. We'd talked about the possibility that I was depressed. I told her I'd been feeling tired and blue and that I'd taken St. John's wort for a few weeks. When I mentioned my pee looked foamy, bubbly like detergent soap suds, she'd insisted we draw labs before treating me for depression.

"What do you mean, 'my kidneys'?" I repeated, confused. All I knew about kidneys was that there were two, located in my back, and that they had something to do with peeing.

"I'm sorry, Lisa, but your lab results show your kidneys are in bad shape. You need to go to the hospital right away so we can run more tests. I've already called and made arrangements for your admission. They're expecting you."

The moment of crisis stands strangely outside of time. One minute, you're doing what you always do, and life moves forward in a succession of now-events, everything happening in the moment. Then the crisis hits, and everything stops. All previous thoughts, habits, all the momentum of life abruptly screeches to a halt.

In a cataclysmic schism, my life split irrevocably in two: the before and the after.

I hung up the phone, finished the follow-up email I'd been working on, and then focused on the logistics of getting to the hospital. I couldn't ride my bike, not if I was sick. Kurt was busy at his startup in the City. I needed my sister to bring our car.

She'd left eight years of peaceful paradise in Hawaii to come and find a job in the booming Bay Area Internet economy. Kurt and I had volunteered our spare bedroom as a launching pad for her new life, and she was borrowing our car to look for work. Fortunately, she was home when I called.

"Hey, Marly Darly, I need you to come get me."

"Lisi, what's wrong?"

"I need you to take me to the hospital." When she made to interrupt, I rushed on. "I'll explain when you get here, but you've got to come now, as fast as you can."

The moment I hung up, I called Kurt.

"Hi, my dear." I tried to sound casual. I didn't want him to worry, especially not until we had a better idea of what was going on, and he had enough to worry about at his job. As it was, I had enough anxiety for the both of us.

"The doctor called and my labs from last week came back a little weird. Marla's going to take me to the hospital so they can run some more tests."

"What was weird? Did the doctor say?"

My tone had worked and he didn't sound overly concerned.

"Something about my kidneys. I'll call you as soon as we know more. I love you." I fought to control my voice and keep the fear out it. My body was shaking.

"I love you, too."

Cara had left for a client meeting, so I would have to tell Helen, my boss, what was going on, but I stood paralyzed for a moment beside the desk. Sweat drenched my armpits while chills shivered through my body. These vague symptoms had been going on for so long I couldn't remember exactly when they started. The sulfurous, vaguely metallic taste flooding my mouth was another story.

I reached into the desk drawer for a stick of strong peppermint gum, when the computer screen caught my eye, reminding me of all the follow-up I had to do. I was under deadline! But I had to get to the hospital. I felt my stress level ratchet up another notch and my heart throbbed uncomfortably as I rushed down the hall to Helen's corner office.

As the founder and president of an up-and-coming high tech PR agency, Helen had always intimidated me with her professional demeanor, her expressionless face, and her poker-like manner. Being a mere account executive, I'd managed to avoid her most of the time and work with Cara, who was my direct superior. Now, I had to face her.

Her door stood open. She was on the phone but quickly noticed me and waved me in. I closed the door behind me and fought to get myself under control. I clenched my teeth, my face tight in an attempt to maintain composure.

She hung up the phone. "What's wrong?"

I wasn't prepared for the unusual concern dawning in her clear blue eyes. I wanted to appear strong and in control—of myself and the situation. I wanted to maintain the persona I'd worked so hard to develop as her employee.

"I've got to go to the hospital right away. Something's wrong with my kidneys..."

My voice died away as I spoke the words. Their import and her atypical sympathy made the gravity of the situation feel all too real. I bowed my head and tried to hide the tears running down my face, my professional demeanor collapsing.

"Of course. Do you need a ride?" She came around the desk with a box of tissues.

"Thanks, but no. My sister's coming with the car. She should be here any minute." I drew a shaky breath. "I don't have time to do the follow up on the EOS release." It felt like a confession of failure.

"Don't worry about that right now, Lisa. Do what you need to do." Her phone started to ring and she went to answer it.

"I'll call you as soon as I know what's going on," I said as I wiped away the tears and headed for the door. She was already on the phone again.

The drive to the hospital was tense. Marla focused on navigating through the thick Berkeley morning traffic and I rattled on in a frenzy of meaningless words, hoping to keep her worry and my own terror at bay. When the words ran out, I stared blankly ahead, the tangle of emotions and memory threatening to overwhelm me.

Something was wrong, really wrong. Was I dying?

The thought of hospitals brought back memories of fatal disease, of death, and of my friend Tom.

He'd been one of my closest friends since my grad school days at UC Santa Barbara, when we'd shared a house for a year. He'd been hospitalized in January for AIDS-related symptoms. The last time I saw him was in April, at his parents' house in the South Bay. He lay in his childhood room in a big metal hospital bed, emaciated, feverish, and very ill. His apartment was gone and his gold Toyota Corolla with the sporty sunroof had been sold. It was obvious he didn't have much longer. He had died in May, just a little over six months before now.

Would my end come like his, swift, horrible, and so unbearably final?

Marla's voice broke into my dark thoughts. "It looks like parking is going to be a real drag. I'll drop you off here so you can start checking in."

We pulled up to the curb at the front of the hospital and I got out.

Admissions

DIALYSIS: A MEMOIR

I'd never been hospitalized before, so walking into Admissions felt unreal and disorienting. It was now 10 a.m. The large room was crowded with a multitude of people who reflected the diversity of Berkeley and Oakland. I ignored the other waiting people and rushed to the nearest of five cubicles adjoining the main room. A well-dressed, older black woman wearing a lot of gold jewelry sat behind the desk. She was speaking to a young pregnant Latina and her husband.

"Excuse me," I said, putting on my most ingratiating smile. "I'm sorry to interrupt, but my doctor told me I need to be admitted right away."

The woman looked unimpressed. "Did you see the clipboard over there?" She pointed across the crowded waiting room. When I shook my head, she continued. "It's on the table by the front door. Put your name on it and we will get to you as soon as we can."

"But my doctor says I have to be admitted right away!" I couldn't believe I'd have to wait.

The woman merely glanced at me over her large, gold-rimmed glasses, her eyes piercing. "As I said, you need to put your name on the waiting list."

Before I could think of a response, the woman resumed speaking to the pregnant woman and her husband.

I hurried over to put my name on the list. I counted the names ahead of me. Fifteen! How long would that take? There wasn't any time to waste! Something was really wrong. The doctor said so. I wanted to go back and argue with the woman, but then I looked around the room. The place was filled with people of different ages, races, and cultures. It dawned on me that many looked worse off than I, so feeling worried and helpless, I found one of the last available chairs and took a seat. It was 10:05 a.m.

By 10:15, Marla showed up.

"Can you believe it took me almost twenty minutes to find street parking? No way was I going to pay the garage parking fee. It was crazy expensive."

"Well, have a seat. We're going to be here a while." I clued her in about the waiting list.

"Are you kidding me?"

"I've made it this far, so I guess I can survive another couple of hours." I joked, trying to lighten the mood.

But I have never been good at waiting. I wanted to jump into action, to do something, anything, to stave off the fear eating at me. Instead, we waited, and I grew increasingly irritated with the hospital admissions process. My world was the snappy, high-efficiency world of Internet business and high tech PR. My specialty was smooth, high-speed productivity. This place plodded along, the epitome of bureaucratic lethargy.

"Did you call Mom and Bob?" Marla asked.

"Not yet." I hadn't thought that far ahead. I was still hoping this was all some kind of terrible mistake.

"Do you want me to go and call them? I'm sure they'll want to know what's going on."

"Sure, if you don't mind. At this rate, you should have plenty of time," I grimaced sarcastically.

Once Marla left in search of a phone (hard to believe life before cell phones!), I grabbed an old issue of People lying among the pile of ratty, outdated magazines on the end table beside me. Desperately, I thumbed through it, but the distraction didn't work. I tried to ignore the people around me, some of whom looked dreadfully ill. The elderly white man across from me wheezed in gasping spurts, as though he couldn't get enough oxygen and might keel over at any moment.

Seeing him reminded me of Tom and how the flesh had hung from his large, emaciated frame. On the heels of that memory came a more distant one, an old man, wizened and ravaged by chemotherapy and cancer, little more than a head on a stick, poking up from thin hospital blankets. Peter had been my boss, mentor, and good friend for three summers during college when I worked in a chemistry lab. He died in December 1987, the year I graduated. I still missed him. And I missed Tom.

DIALYSIS: A MEMOIR

Where did death fit amidst the infinite energy, youth and possibility of the Internet boom in the Bay Area? Money seemed to pour from the skies, SUVs grew bigger, semiconductors shrank smaller and computed faster. Nothing died or ended, it was simply retooled and released as a new version. Or you found another venture capitalist to back your idea. Because of the friends I'd lost and now this illness, my personal experience felt completely at odds with the euphoria around me.

I stared at the magazine in my lap and tried to diagnose my symptoms. The cold yet sweaty sensations and foamy pee had been going on for a while, but the disgusting taste in my mouth had just started on Saturday.

Kurt and I'd had sushi with Marla and Kurt's cousin in Japantown that night. After dinner, as we sat in his cousin's apartment listening to him play guitar, a vile taste suddenly flooded my mouth and I began to burp revolting, nauseating burps. That was the first time I felt, deep in my gut, that something was terribly wrong.

Did I have kidney cancer? Was I going to die?

No! I refused to believe it. I come from a long line of powerful women. My mother forged her way in the male-dominated world of the hard sciences and made a name for herself. At eight-seven, my grandmother still persisted, refusing to relent to death. My great grandmother lived to one hundred and two, my great-great grandmother to one hundred. No one in my immediate family had ever become seriously sick before their seventies, and none of us had ever had kidney problems.

I'd always assumed that I'd live to a ripe old age. But what if all that history meant nothing in my case? What if I was the exception to the rule?

Tears welled up, but then Marla came back and took the now empty seat beside me.

"They're making arrangements to fly out," she said.

"Really? But what if this all turns out to be nothing?" Some part of me still clung to hope, or was it denial?

"Lisi, you're being admitted into the hospital. Mom says they'll be here as soon as possible. I told Mom I'd call again tonight, once we know what's going on." She took my hands in hers, her blue eyes rimmed with red. "This is so crazy. What's happening to you?"

"I don't know." I put the magazine back on the side table and scowled. "I hate hospitals. Do you remember that time we went to see Mom after her hysterectomy? And then there was that time Dad was hospitalized."

"When was Dad in the hospital?"

"When I was six, I think, but I don't remember why."

"I don't remember that. Are you going to call him?"

"I don't know. Maybe later."

There were bigger things on my mind at the moment than notifying my father, especially given the minimalist nature of our relationship. My parents divorced when I was twelve, and he'd basically walked out of my life on my fifteenth birthday, when he announced he was moving to Pennsylvania with his new family.

Someone called my name. It was 11:05 a.m., more than an hour after I'd arrived. I hurried forward, anxious to finally get started. The same woman I'd spoken with earlier processed my paperwork. She made copies of my insurance card and I gave her the medical history and emergency contact forms I'd filled out. She clamped a plastic bracelet on my wrist with my identity and allergy information on it, handed me my chart, and then perfunctorily directed me to the Oncology Unit.

Stunned speechless, my heart clenched with dread. Were my fears justified? Did I really have cancer?

Day One

"'Oncology' means cancer, right?" Marla asked as we rode the elevator to the hospital's fourth floor. When I nodded, she said, "Why are they putting you in the Cancer Unit?"

"Good question. I guess we'll find out soon enough." I tried to sound calm, but I had a sick feeling in my stomach.

We pushed through a set of heavy double doors into Oncology. The unit was designed like a wheel. Numerous halls radiated out from the central hub, which housed a huge desk where many nurses and other staff congregated. I approached the desk. A perky brunette nurse in pale blue scrubs looked up and smiled. I handed her my folder of information. She snapped it open and quickly scanned the first page.

"Hello, Lisa," she said. "We've been expecting you. Please come this way."

Marla and I followed her down one of the halls. As we walked, I dared to ask the dreaded question.

"Do you know why I'm in the Oncology Unit?"

"Nephrology's all booked up. They're just across the way from us here on the fourth floor, but they have absolutely no space right now."

I tuned out the rest of what she was saying and breathed a huge sigh of relief. Whatever was wrong with me, it wasn't cancer. As Marla and I followed her into one of the hospital rooms, I was thinking that nothing could be as bad as cancer.

"Here's your room," the nurse said as we entered. "You'll have to share with Sister Mikki. Her real name is Sister Maureen O'Geary, but everybody calls her Sister Mikki."

The nurse gestured to a bald, elderly woman lying in the bed by the door. Sister Mikki was on the phone and didn't acknowledge us.

"Here's your bed and here are your robes. Put one on facing front and the other facing back. That way, you'll be all covered up."

The nurse glanced at my chart.

"Dr. Pali has been assigned to your case. She's an excellent nephrologist. Judging from her orders, it looks like you'll have a series of tests today and then she'll check in with you tomorrow, once the results are back. Oh, and before I forget, put your street clothes and other belongings in this bag. We can put any valuables in the hospital safe."

She handed me a large plastic bag and then hurried away.

I looked at Marla. "Now what?"

"I guess we'll find out." She sat down on the one chair on my side of the room.

Sister Mikki was still on the phone on the other side of the thin, salmon-colored curtain that separated the two halves of the room. While I changed into the hospital gowns and slipped into the pair of beige, anti-slip hospital socks, I couldn't help but listen to her, since she was practically shouting.

"No, no, no, Sally, you did not hear me correctly. I said, I will not be able to leave here for another week." She painstakingly articulated each word, like she was speaking to someone hard of hearing. "Yes, it is a terrible trial. Can you believe that, Sally? Four weeks in the hospital! It is unbelievable what they are putting me through. And Sally, let me tell you, I have not had a single good night's sleep here. What was that, Sally?"

Marla and I looked at each other, and I wondered how long I was going to have to be in the hospital.

A good-looking, black orderly appeared with a gurney.

"You've got a date with X-Ray. Climb on." He pulled the blanket aside and slipped the straps of the gurney free.

"Why can't I walk?" I was perfectly capable of walking, and I wanted to preserve whatever sense of independence I had left.

"Hospital procedure. Now climb on." He looked at his watch. "I gotta get you across the hospital and down to the basement. I'm running late."

"Can I come?" Marla asked as he fastened the straps and laid a blanket over me.

"Nah. You can wait here or in the lobby." He started to push me down the hall.

"How long will it take?" Marla called out after us.

The orderly shrugged and kept moving, "Dunno."

DIALYSIS: A MEMOIR

The next few hours passed in a blur. First came the chest X-ray, then I was sent for a kidney ultrasound, and then an MRI. In between procedures, I was rolled into the hall and left waiting on the gurney for the next orderly to come and wheel me to the next destination.

I wasn't alone. Several other gurneys also waited alongside the hallway walls. All I could see from my vantage point was the white-haired head of a patient on the one and the beige hospital socks of the patient on the other. Neither moved much. I assumed they were asleep, though the white-haired patient periodically coughed. I lay on the gurney and shivered in the thin cotton hospital robes under the meager blanket. My watch was back in the plastic bag in the hospital room. I had no way of telling how much time passed.

I lay passive, exhausted, and stared up at the textured white ceiling tiles and fluorescent lights, clenching and unclenching my teeth when the next round of chills seized me. Without all the demands of everyday life to distract me, I experienced the full extent of my bodily deterioration. I was cold, sick, tired, and barely hanging on.

How had it come to this?

Just a few weeks ago, Cara and I had agreed that during the holiday season we'd run at lunch to work off the extra calories. Our jobs were exciting and intense, and all too often we'd work through lunch and not stop to take time out from the whirlwind.

But that Wednesday, we had. The run was a flat one, only about a mile around the Emeryville marina and back. It was one of those spectacularly clear California winter days, the landforms magnified by the lack of a marine layer and the colors enhanced by the crystalline quality of the pristine air. San Francisco rose like Oz, tall and glittery above the steel blue bay to the west. The Golden Gate Bridge glowed red. Mount Tam loomed dark, unconquered and uncivilized to the north. The beauty meant nothing to me as I ruthlessly pushed through the fatigue and pain to keep pace with Cara.

By the end of the run, my legs were cramping. By the time we reached the last flight of stairs leading to our office, I could barely walk. I masked the pain with a laugh and told Cara to go ahead, that I needed time to stretch. Once she'd left, I grasped the banister to hoist myself up the last flight. With each step, my legs cramped furiously and I panted for breath. When I finally reached my office, I could do nothing but close the door and lie under my desk, cold, cramping, sweaty, and hoping that no one would notice. Even in high school, when I was forty pounds heavier and completely out of shape, I could have easily run that flat, little distance. That's when I realized that what was wrong with me might not just be in my mind. I called the doctor that afternoon.

"You look like you could use a warm blanket." An orderly pushing a large cart stopped, pulled out a blanket, and spread it over me.

"Thanks." I smiled up at the man and huddled under the intense, comforting heat. I'd never heard of heated blankets before, but what an excellent idea! If only someone would bring me another when this one cooled. But no one did. Instead, another indefinite period passed and my chills returned full force.

Suddenly, I found myself looking up at Marla, my sister to the rescue.

"Hey Sis, you done with the tests, right?" She smiled down at me.

"Yes." My teeth were chattering.

"So what are you doing here?"

"Waiting for someone to take me back to my room." I was too cold and tired to ask how she'd found me.

"How long have you been waiting?" She looked at the empty hall. The other gurneys had disappeared.

"Too long. Get me out of here."

We rode the service elevator up to the fourth floor, giggling, perhaps a little hysterically, that we'd exerted some small control over the situation and the hospital's bureaucratic inefficiency. She wheeled me back to Oncology, and we made it in time for the last part of my favorite soap, General Hospital.

The latest drama managed to distract me for a time, despite the fact that Sister Mikki's current phone conversation was audible over the TV's small, movable speaker, which I placed by my head with the volume on high. Interesting how something so inane and trivial as a soap opera could help me cope, but it came as a wonderful relief to imagine someone else's life—a fictional person's story that, no matter how wild and crazy, always turned out OK in the end.

A nurse came in shortly after the show ended to take my vitals. I decided it was time to exert a little more control over my situation.

"Do you know when I'll see a doctor?" I asked.

"Probably not until tomorrow," she said as she wrote my blood pressure values in the chart.

"What?" I couldn't believe it. Who was overseeing my care?

"The nephrology team has already done their rounds for the day. It looks here," she glanced at the chart, "like you're scheduled for several more procedures tomorrow."

"How long do I have to stay in the hospital?"

"You'll have to ask the docs when you see them."

After the nurse left, Marla brought a few more blankets to lay over me.

"You'll be OK," she said. Her eyes were big and blue, slightly teary, and her nose was red and swollen. She was so caring, so beautiful, and so scared.

"I guess we'll have to wait for tomorrow to get some answers." I had to give Helen an update, and I wondered what I should tell her.

"I've got a job interview at 4." Marla looked at her watch. "Should I cancel it?"

"Of course not. I'll call Kurt. You go."

"You sure?"

"Hey, what could happen? I'm in a hospital, right?" I tried to lighten the situation. I was her big sister, after all, and she'd already done enough.

She gave me a hug before she left.

I called Helen, but it was with some relief that I reached our office administrator instead. She told me Helen was out at a client meeting, so I gave her a quick status update to pass along and then prepared myself to call Kurt.

Ever since our first meeting on the bike team in grad school nine years earlier, Kurt and my relationship had been predicated on our being two separate, independent, and self-sufficient individuals, coming together to share good times. We'd always kept our relationship emotionally and physically ordered. We avoided drama and we'd developed a routine of hard physical exercise, lots of good food, and great sex.

Like my parents, his had split up in the seventies, but the destructive forces in his family were nothing like mine. His dad abandoned them in Indianapolis to go to Chicago and become a gay artist. His mom was later hospitalized for schizophrenia, and his brother and he spent several years collecting the welfare checks and living on their own. Perhaps it was no surprise that he and his brother studied mathematics. Its logical order and established rules of engagement must have been a welcome relief after the chaos of their childhood.

I was not consciously aware of how this history influenced my behavior with him, but undoubtedly, I must have feared that if I revealed my weakness to him, he like his dad and mine might leave.

"Hey, my dear." I kept my voice strong, not worried I'd bother Sister Mikki, since she was hard of hearing. "I've been admitted to the hospital."

"What? I thought they were just going to run some tests."

"They did, but they needed to admit me as part of the process."

"Does that mean you'll have to spend the night?"

"Yes. I have to have some more procedures tomorrow, too." I looked at the clock on the wall. It was 3:30 pm.

"I'll be there as soon as I can," he said.

His words reassured me, and after I hung up, I fell asleep.

When I awoke, he was there. He came and sat on the bed.

"I brought my sleeping bag and mat." He gestured to the gear on the floor between the bed and the window. "I'm going to spend the night, and I'm taking tomorrow off work."

"Is that OK with your boss?"

"He's fine with it."

"Do you think it'll be OK with the hospital if you spend the night?"

"I don't care. I'm staying." He stood up and unrolled his sleeping mat.

"Thanks." I watched him and wiped away tears. It was a relief to know he'd be there beside me.

For dinner, he brought in a deli sandwich and I picked at the lousy hospital meatloaf and watery mashed potatoes. Even if the food had been a gourmet delicacy, I would have been repulsed. The illness that had encroached on my life had killed my appetite.

After dinner, Kurt lay down in his sleeping bag. Neither of us wanted to talk about the day that had passed or worry aloud about what was to come. The sweet unconsciousness of sleep seemed the best plan of action. Sister Mikki was silent on her side of the room.

I couldn't sleep. The cold fatigue sank down over my body and the sulfurous taste infected my mouth. Kurt's light breathing deepened as he drifted off. Sister Mikki tossed and turned on the other side of the curtain. Random sounds of nurses and rolling equipment echoed in the hallway. I lay in that place between wakefulness and sleep and remembered my life before everything slipped away.

Just six months ago, I'd been a blonde Amazon. Biking, running, backpacking, I'd matched Kurt stride for stride. Fourth of July weekend, we'd set off with two of his Cornell buddies on a cross-country backpacking route through a remote region of the Emigrant Wilderness north of Yosemite.

We left the civilized comfort of hiking on the dirt road and plunged off-trail through steep, sloping underbrush and pine trees. I led the way and navigated a route across the difficult terrain. For three hours, we sweated up inclines and the guys groaned down the descents, their packs heavy and their knees straining under the load. Undaunted by the physical exertion, I gloried in the fierce strength of my powerful legs and the enormous capacity of my lungs to move my body with ease across the land. When the others stopped to cross-check our progress against the topo map and take a brief rest to eat trail mix and Clif Bars, I charged ahead, relying purely on my navigational instinct.

Before me lay the final ascent, a granite dome looming several hundred feet above. I hitched the pack higher on my back and my legs surged with energy as I began the climb. My breath came easily and my footing was sure and quick on the rough granite. The trees fell away. The sky blazed bright blue and cloudless. I summited and gazed in wonder at the vast vista spread out before me, a world of rock and water. The High Sierra beckoned on the horizon—treeless, stark, and white. Below me lay the swimming hole, the waterfalls, and the campsite. I sat on the smooth, glacier-worn granite, munched a delicious brownie, and waited for the others. The future lay ahead, an adventure filled with exciting possibilities.

Sister Mikki groaned loudly and the glorious dream dissolved. I glanced at the clock on the bedside stand: 11 p.m. I peered over the edge of the bed. Kurt was still asleep. I lay back against the pillow and wished Sister Mikki would be quiet, but her groans grew louder. Kurt's hand came up and took mine. I rolled over and looked down at him in the dim light.

He smiled, squeezed my hand, and then pulled his fleece jacket over his head to muffle the noise.

I tried putting the extra hospital pillow over my head, but now that I was fully awake, I couldn't go back to sleep. I lay there, exhausted, and numbly listened to Sister Mikki's vocal suffering.

At midnight, she buzzed the nurse. When no one responded, she began shouting, "Nurse! Nurse! Someone please help me. Please!"

The nurse finally arrived, tended to Sister Mikki, and then came to take my blood pressure and temperature.

In the quiet that followed, I finally drifted off. But then at 2 a.m., another voice woke us.

"Sir, sir, you can't stay here!"

We looked up into the distressed eyes of a Filipina nurse. She frowned down at Kurt.

"What do you mean? I'm here with my wife." He sat up and in doing so exposed his naked chest.

The nurse's eyebrows shot higher.

"Heavens no! You can't sleep in the same room as the Sister." The nurse whispered frantically and pointed to the curtain.

Kurt's lips set firmly. "Then she can leave." He started to get up.

The nurse backed away, shocked, and shook her head desperately. "No, no. Please, cover yourself." She rushed from the room.

"I'm not leaving." Kurt looked up at me.

"I'm glad. But what if they try to make you leave?"

"Don't worry. Let's try to get some more sleep."

We lay back down.

About a half hour later, the nurse returned and woke us up again.

Her face was grim, but resigned. "There are no other free rooms tonight," she said, "so you can stay. But only tonight."

Thanks to the tepid charity of the night nurse and Sister Mikki's extra heavy dose of sleeping pills or pain medication or whatever it was that kept her from groaning and buzzing the nurse, Kurt and I managed exactly four hours of sleep. Then the morning nurse arrived.

Chapter 2 - Kidney Failure

Tuesday

The morning nurse came at 6 a.m. to stick me for some more lab work. She mentioned that someone would be along shortly to "Cut you and measure your bleeding time." Kurt and I were appalled. How medieval! It sounded like using leeches for bloodletting.

The man who came to do the cutting was perfunctorily friendly.

"This won't take but a minute," he said. He unrolled a small cloth and placed his shiny steel implements on it.

"Why are you doing this?" I still couldn't believe he was about to cut me on the forearm with what looked like some kind of razor.

"This is the quickest and most effective way to measure your clotting ability, even in this modern day and age. Here goes." He laid the razor against my skin.

After all the needle poking I'd endured over the past twelve hours, being cut with a razor didn't hurt that much, just the cool sensation of steel sliding against skin, a pause, and then a brief sting when the cut came in contact with the disinfectant. I couldn't watch the cutting. I looked out the window and noticed that Kurt had also turned his head away.

"How did I do?" I asked the man as he gathered his tools.

"Just fine." He hurried from the room before either Kurt or I thought to ask him why my bleeding time needed to be measured.

Marla arrived soon after with a bag of bagels and coffee.

"Thought you might want some breakfast," she said to Kurt. She pulled the small table closer to the bed and arranged the bagels and spreads on it.

"Awesome." Kurt moved the chair to the table and sat down.

Marla slid over the chair from Sister Mikki's side of the room, since the nun wasn't there. She'd been wheeled away by an orderly for some reason.

Another orderly brought my breakfast, but the soggy pancakes and greasy sausage looked disgusting. I picked at it, not hungry and still feeling wiped out after my night in the hospital and the events of the previous day.

A doctor with long, flowing black hair and high-heeled pumps clicked into the room. She wore an electric blue dress suit beneath a white lab coat.

"Good day, I am Dr. Pali." She spoke with a strong Indian accent as she shook my hand. Hers was cool and dry, with dark red-painted nails. She spoke quickly and got straight to the point, foregoing any polite preliminaries.

"I am the nephrologist overseeing your case, Lisa. It is unfortunate but the results of the diagnostic tests we ran yesterday do not look good. I am particularly concerned about your lab values. Your creatinine was off-scale and your BUN was ninety-five. This is severely abnormal. Many of your other kidney values were also elevated and your hematocrit was badly depressed." She paused for a moment, frowning.

The technical terms meant nothing to me and her heavy accent made them sound even more alien. I stared blankly at her.

"I am sorry to be the bearer of bad news," she continued, "but based on these results, I have determined that your kidneys are failing."

My kidneys failing? Impossible! I knew I was sick, but organ failure seemed too disastrous, too catastrophic. I wasn't thinking clearly enough to stop her and ask for definitions of the medical terminology. Her words bombarded me in a barrage of information.

"You need to begin dialysis immediately. It will cleanse your blood and help purge your body of toxins, which will make you feel much better. We will give you a permacatheter to get you started on dialysis. Let's hope this is a case of acute nephritis and we won't have to give you something more permanent. If it turns out you do have end stage renal disease, however, we will need to implant a fistula into your forearm. Of course, you might prefer peritoneal dialysis—"

Her words hit me like bullets and finally ripped through the blankness that had momentarily paralyzed me. Before she could say anything more, I retched and spilled the meager remains of my breakfast onto the blanket covering my lap as the world went black.

"Oh my God, Lisi! What's wrong with her?" Marla's voice came through the thick cold fog enshrouding me.

"This often happens in cases of severe stress. She will be fine." Dr. Pali did not sound worried.

I opened my eyes and saw Kurt bringing in a clean blanket. He laid it across me and gave me a quiet smile. He took my hand and sat beside me on the bed. We turned to face Dr. Pali.

"Except for your kidneys, you are young and healthy, so you should be an excellent candidate for a transplant. The kidney biopsy I have arranged for you today will tell us definitively whether or not your kidney failure is acute. The tests of the biopsied material will also give us a good idea of what caused your condition. In the meantime, I will have one of the nurses give you a tour of the dialysis unit this morning so you can become familiar with it. Do you have any questions?" She finally stopped speaking.

"Do you?" Kurt squeezed my hand.

"Not now." I shrugged still feeling like hell.

Dr. Pali left the room. Kurt and Marla discussed what the doctor had said, but I lay back against the hospital pillows and closed my eyes.

Under normal circumstances, I would have appreciated Dr. Pali's quick, efficient and business-like information dump. After all, this was something I valued in my own professional life. Normally, I would have wanted to be given as much information as possible about my medical condition and treatment options. At the moment, however, with my body cold and sweaty and my mouth full of bile, I wasn't ready to hear everything.

Promptly following Dr. Pali's visit, an orderly brought a wheelchair to take me to the dialysis unit. Kurt and Marla came along. A dialysis nurse introduced herself to us in the hall outside and escorted us inside. None of us had ever been in a dialysis unit, and until that morning, I'd never even heard the word "dialysis" before.

Nothing prepared me for what I was about to see. The nightmare vision seemed like something from a second-rate horror movie, with patients lying helpless, bloodlines coming and going from their arms to giant machines. The room reeked, a disturbing mix of alcohol, vinegar, and other evil-smelling chemicals, and it was noisy, the beeping of alarms, the cacophony of the TVs bolted to the ceiling, the repetitive sounds of the machines pumping the blood through the tubes to the patients. I heard nothing the nurse was saying. In moments, my world went black again. I collapsed out of the wheelchair and onto the floor.

"Oh dear, the poor girl!" I heard the nurse's concerned voice and felt hands gripping me sturdily under the arms.

"I'm OK," I mumbled while the orderly and Kurt reseated me in the wheelchair.

"That's enough of a tour for now," the nurse said. "You'll be back this afternoon to start your dialysis."

It was a relief when Kurt wheeled me back to the hospital room. If Marla and he were as appalled by the dialysis unit as I was, I couldn't tell. My own feelings of utter devastation obliterated all else from my mind.

Manuel Junior

Less than an hour later, an orderly came to take me for the permacatheter surgery.

"Don't worry." Kurt kissed me. "We'll be here when you get back."

The orderly pushed me down the hall and into the service elevator. I spent the elevator ride trying to bribe myself that if I could just get through the procedure I'd reward myself with my soap opera. Following on the heels of that thought, however, came the worry that the procedure might take too long and I'd miss my show.

The orderly wheeled me out of the elevator and down a hall to a room that reverberated with rock and roll music. Nurses, doctors, and other assorted staff bustled about, dressed in either white or blue scrubs, speaking loudly over the music. The pulsing rhythm shook the room and throbbed through my cold, tired body, beating down the fear and anxiety I felt at seeing the operating theater with its glistening, stainless steel surgical equipment and myriad machines. Instead, when the nurses helped me onto the operating gurney, I lay back, quiescent, unable to do anything more than shiver and smile wanly at the people hurrying about their business and hooking me up to the machines.

The nurse who was hooking me up to a blood pressure cuff and pulse rate monitor shouted across the room. "Hey, turn it down a sec, OK?"

The music abruptly stopped. The nurse smiled down at me, her brown eyes friendly behind thick glasses.

"As you can see, we do things a little differently here. We've found that patients are more relaxed during surgery if they can listen to music. And," she winked at me, "we like it, too. So, do you have any requests?"

Peace and quiet would have been nice. Instead, I said, "How about the Blues? Do you have any Muddy Waters?" When the nurse looked blank, I said, "How about some Jazz? Do you have any Coltrane or Miles Davis?"

The nurse on my other side piped up. "You know we've never had a request for Blues or Jazz before! I think the closest thing we've got is Bonnie Raitt. Would that work?"

I nodded, but without enthusiasm. Not that I don't like Bonnie Raitt, but it was hard to muster excitement about the musical selection at the moment.

"Hey, can you put on the Bonnie Raitt album?" The first nurse yelled.

In seconds, Bonnie's voice swelled and filled the room, singing of love and the green-forested mountains of Appalachia.

"I'm going to get you set up for the anesthesia." The second nurse spoke loudly over the music. "Turn your head hard to the left. A bit more. More. OK, keep it there."

My neck screamed in protest at being twisted sideways to such a severe angle. Out of the corner of my right eye, I saw the first nurse standing over me with long needles that she was jamming into the right side of my neck. Meanwhile, the second nurse pushed a two-pronged, plastic tube into my nostrils.

"This might tickle a little and it may feel dry," she said. "It's oxygen. Just make sure to keep breathing through your nose."

While all this was going on, I glimpsed a doctor in white scrubs approaching.

"Hi everybody! Hi Lisa, how are you today?" The doctor's teeth looked very white as he smiled down at me. "I'm Dr. Manuel Caruño and I'm going to give you a 'Manuel Junior'. Hey, is this Bonnie Raitt? An excellent choice! What a beautiful voice she has! Did you choose her?"

Under different circumstances, I might have thought it strange, his naming the permacatheter after himself, but I had little bandwidth for reflection. Dr. Caruño had me hostage, lying prostrate on the hospital gurney with my neck twisted so far to the left that I could barely see him, and with the tubes up my nose, I was afraid to respond to him for fear of dislodging them.

"OK everybody, let's get this party started!" he shouted.

Dr. Caruño and his team sprang into action. The discomfort from my twisted neck and from the anesthesia needles couldn't compare with the intense pain Dr. Caruño began to inflict. From the edge of my vision, I could see him standing over me and pushing with all his might to stab something into my chest cavity. There was something hideously intimate about a procedure being conducted so close to my face while I was still conscious. Nurses stood on either side of me, and Dr. Caruño stood somehow above me, doing something I couldn't quite see, periodically muttering through the surgical mask, "Everything's going to be fine. Everything's going to be just great. I'm giving you a Manuel Junior."

I tried to focus on Bonnie Raitt and the soothing strains of her music. As I lay there feeling like it was the end of the world, I tried to picture beautiful things in my mind, places I had been, both real and imaginary. I reached back into my past to the scene I'd creatively visualized during est (Erhard Seminar Training) in my early teens. I tried as hard as I could to envision myself standing on that white, sandy beach with a line of spectacular waves breaking perfectly in the distance. I tried to focus on the swell of Bonnie's voice and the melody of the tune, the blue-green beauty of my imaginary sea. I tried to remove myself from the present moment, but it didn't work. My body felt like it was shutting down, like I was dying.

"Hey, what's happening?!" One nurse shouted over the music.

"Her pulse rate has dropped to thirty, blood pressure eighty over forty." The other nurse relayed the information from the digital readouts.

"She's having a vasovagal response, poor girl. She must be very sick." Dr. Caruño's voice came from somewhere above, and for a moment, the horrible pressure on my chest eased.

"Breathe, Lisa. It's OK. Breathe. There you go." The nurse on my left squeezed my hand in reassurance.

The pressure resumed briefly, and then it was all over, an enormous ice pack pressed hard against my right upper chest and shoulder.

"Great job, everybody! And congratulations to you, Lisa!" Dr. Caruño removed his face mask and his white smile gleamed. "You have a beautiful Manuel Junior. I'm sorry it hurt so much, but we usually insert permacaths into older folks, who don't have a lot of muscle. Their skin is papery thin and easy to penetrate. Your skin was young and very tight, and you have a lot of muscle mass in your chest cavity that I had to push through. But we succeeded! Your Manuel Junior is going to work like a charm."

Dr. Caruño spoke with a paternal pride that might have appalled me under other circumstances, but as it was, I couldn't let myself think about what had just happened. I looked at the clock on the wall, instead, and worried that I might miss my soap opera.

Another orderly arrived to wheel me off for my first dialysis session and Bonnie Raitt's voice suddenly stopped. Silence filled the operating theater. And then, as if on cue, Mick Jagger belted out the first few lines of the Rolling Stones' song, "Shattered."

Hemodialysis

I made it to the dialysis unit in time for my show, but then I wasn't able to focus on the TV bolted to the ceiling above my bed. There was too much going on around me. When the nurse prepared to hook me up to the dialysis machine, I began to cry.

"Here, you gotta wear this." The nurse smiled sympathetically and handed me a paper face mask. She pulled on latex gloves and donned a face mask herself.

I blinked away the tears, not wanting to appear weak or overemotional.

From what I could see, the permacath consisted of a small, white plastic oval piece implanted in my upper chest below my clavicle and connected to two, six-inch long tubes that hung downward. The two tubes were taped together and each ended in a different color cap. One had a red end and the other had blue to indicate which connected to my arterial and my venous blood lines.

The nurse popped off the disposable caps on each lead, momentarily exposing my blood to the open air, and then connected each to the tubes running to the dialysis machine.

I watched in horrified fascination as the blood flowed out of my body toward the machine. At the same instant, I felt a cool sensation flooding through my body. The nurse noticed my surprised expression.

"You're feeling the saline solution we use to prep the lines. Don't worry. It'll last just a moment. The dialysis machine will warm up your blood so that when it comes back into your body it won't feel so cold."

I nodded, but as I watched my blood return from the machine and flow back into my body, I started to cry again.

Was I really lying in a hospital room along with several old and sickly patients, all of us hooked up to machines we needed in order to stay alive?

I tried to block out everything and focus on the fictional world of General Hospital. Luke and Laura's relationship was on the rocks again. Several minutes later, a balding doctor approached carrying my chart.

"Hello, Lisa, I'm with Dr. Pali's nephrology group. How's your first dialysis going?"

Although he seemed kind and appeared concerned, I vaguely resented his intrusion. Laura was about to reveal her feelings for Stefan, a Cassidine and Luke's arch nemesis. I wanted to see Luke's reaction, but I was too tired to resent his intrusion with any intensity.

"I'm doing OK, I guess." I shrugged and kept watching the TV.

"Do you mind if I take a look at your permacatheter?"

I shrugged again, but to be polite, I tried to muster a smile. "Sure."

He leaned over and pulled back my hospital gown to more clearly examine where the permacath entered my chest.

"Dr. Caruño has done an excellent job. With luck this permacath should last at least three months without complications. We can decide then whether to implant a more permanent access. While you're in the hospital, we'll dialyze you every day to help stabilize your lab values and bring your creatinine down. That should make you feel much better. Once you're released from the hospital, you'll only need to be dialyzed three times a week."

I wasn't prepared to think about leaving the hospital, and I was getting very thirsty.

"Could you bring me some water?" I croaked as the doctor prepared to leave.

"No," he shook his head. "I'm sorry, but the purpose of dialysis is to remove excess fluid from your blood. I'll have the nurse bring you some ice chips. Sucking on those should help relieve your dry mouth."

Besides giving me severe dry mouth, the dialysis made me feel chilled, and very light-headed and woozy. I huddled under the thin hospital blanket and fell asleep before the ice chips arrived. Ironically, though the anticipation of seeing my favorite soap opera had helped get me through the permacath insertion, I ended up sleeping through most of the show.

Kayla Mason

After dialysis, the orderly surprised me by wheeling me past Oncology and down the hall to a room in the Nephrology Unit. He pushed me past a woman asleep in the first bed to the bed by the window. Kurt was there.

"Long time no see," he said, rising to help me from the wheelchair and into bed. "Room opened up in the Nephrology Unit, so they moved you over here. She doesn't look as bad as Sister Mikki," he whispered and gestured toward the partitioning curtain. "I'd still like to get us our own room."

"What a day," I sighed and lay back against the pillows. I showed him the new appliance dangling from my chest, but I didn't tell him about Dr. Caruño, Manuel Junior, or the permacatheter insertion procedure. He didn't need to know about all that, and I didn't want to relive the experience by talking about it. Instead, I promptly fell asleep.

A while later, the Nephrology Unit's nutritionist, a thin, athletic-looking woman, came to educate me about my new dietary restrictions. She brought a folder of handouts and a book, When Your Kidneys Fail. She described a "renal diet" in great detail, explaining how a kidney friendly diet focuses on optimizing protein intake but limiting salt, phosphorus and potassium.

"Your kidneys are the chemists of your body," she said. "They constantly make adjustments to your blood to make sure your body stays in balance. When they don't work anymore, you have to take charge and really control what you eat and drink. You'll especially need to be careful not to become fluid-overloaded. Understand?"

I nodded.

"Once you're out of the hospital, you'll only be dialyzed every other day, so you'll have to limit your fluid intake to forty ounces each day. And remember, anything that becomes liquid at room temperature is also considered a fluid, so things like popsicles and jello are also fluids."

As she continued to introduce me to a whole new world of eating rules, restrictions, and adjustments that would be my way of life on dialysis, I spaced out. I wasn't ready to think about all the ways my life would change because of kidney failure.

After she left, several of my co-workers came for a brief visit. Their reactions to seeing me in a hospital bed, dressed in a hospital gown, varied. Helen and our office manager seemed completely relaxed and at home, offering me books to read, making jokes, and admiring the floral bouquets sent from friends and family. The vast number of flowers triggered Cara's allergies and she had to run from the room due to a violent allergy attack.

Two other co-workers weren't so comfortable. They had always tended toward being reserved and coolly poised, but now their faces seemed frozen too tightly and their mouths strained to crack smiles. Their eyes flitted uncomfortably about the room, then back and forth across my body, but they didn't meet my eyes. After a few minutes, one of them mumbled an unintelligible apology and left the room.

Only then did it occur to me to consider what I must look like to other young, healthy people. I'd been so wrapped up in my own experience that I hadn't thought of myself as a patient per se, a person in a hospital, sick with a disease, and undergoing a series of medical procedures. Their reactions reminded me of how I used to feel when I came in contact with sick people—a little uneasy, perhaps concerned about contagion.

I dozed after they left and when I next awoke, it was dark outside. I wondered where Kurt had gone, so I got up. As I passed my roommate, she inched herself higher in bed, her hospital gown falling off one shoulder.

"You doing OK? You had a good rest? My poor child, you still look tired." Her short Afro was unstyled, and when she smiled at me, I saw she had one gold front tooth.

"Yes, I'm pretty exhausted," I said.

"You so young to be in the hospital. If you don't mind my asking, whatcha doing in here?"

Feeling dead in my legs, I propped myself against the arm of the chair on her side of the room. I let out a breath and answered. "My kidneys have failed."

I didn't have the energy to feel anything at the moment, and I wasn't ready to admit to myself that what I said was really true. I uttered the words as straight fact, without emotion. The woman had no such reservation.

"Lord have mercy!" She pressed her hand to her chest and her eyes widened in surprise. "But you so young! You don't have no kids, do you?" When I shook my head no, she rushed on in sympathy. "My poor child. I be in this here hospital for the same reason as you. My kidneys done failed and I been here almost three weeks. But the Lord blessed me and I already have my four babies. You so young!" She held out her hand. "I'm Kayla."

I wasn't ready to accept sympathy. To do so would risk too much. I deflected her attention by standing up and moving to shake her hand.

"I'm Lisa. I'm sorry to hear about your kidneys. It must be hard on your family. Are you on dialysis?" Her hand felt cold and dry in mine, but her grip was strong.

"Heavens no! I don't need no dialysis, no matter what them doctors be saying." Kayla's voice shook with the force of her conviction. "I be praying mightily to the Lord and He gonna fix my kidneys. I got faith. He gonna help me."

I was flabbergasted. It had never occurred to me to refuse medical treatment.

"Um, I hope that helps." I didn't know what to say. "I just had my first dialysis this afternoon and it made me really tired."

"You don't need no dialysis!"

When she made to continue her argument, I interrupted, heading for the hall door. "You haven't seen my husband, have you?"

Kayla wasn't offended. "He left a few minutes ago."

I saw Kurt in the hall, headed my way with Marla and one of Kurt's old college friends, who was carrying their dinner in an assortment of bags.

We sat down to our respective dinners, but Kayla didn't turn out to be the quiet patient Kurt had initially assumed.

While we sat on our side of the room speaking softly to each other, Kayla's husband and their four kids, ages four through ten, arrived, carting bags of McDonald's.

I picked at my bland, "renal-friendly" dinner—unsalted chicken breast with overcooked peas and plain pasta—intended to optimize my kidneyless health, but I could smell the enticing, greasy decadence wafting through the thin curtain. Kayla exclaimed in delight over a Big Mac.

It appalled me that the hospital staff allowed her to eat such non-renal-friendly food, especially after the lecture I'd gotten from the nutritionist, but then I realized that patient compliance was something the hospital could encourage but not actually enforce.

From what I could hear, it sounded like one of her sons happily polished off her renal dinner and an extra helping of fries.

Soon after, the curtain wiggled. A small head poked through and an animated little girl looked curiously at the platter of sushi that Kurt and the others were finishing. An older brother's head promptly appeared above hers. He smiled impishly at us.

"You get back here!" Kayla's husband yelled, and the two heads abruptly disappeared.

As the evening wore on, the curtain moved about wildly, and at least two of the kids were involved in some kind of brawl on the floor. The grunts and groans of a sibling squabble reverberated through the room.

"Behave!" Kayla demanded.

The pandemonium continued.

Finally, Kurt couldn't take it anymore. He went in search of a nurse who, as soon as she saw the mayhem, took it upon herself to find us a private room. At long last, Kurt and I had our own place and some peace and quiet.

A Second Chance

First thing Wednesday morning, an orderly arrived and wheeled me off to my next dialysis. About an hour into the three hour process, I suddenly grew voraciously hungry.

As I lay there with my stomach gnawing and growling, I realized I couldn't remember the last time I'd actually felt hungry. Over the past few months, I'd eaten out of habit and routine, not because I desired food but because it was what I was supposed to do. As my kidneys stopped functioning, my body slowly filled with toxins, which killed my appetite.

Now, as the artificial kidney cleansed my blood, my body grew ravenous for nourishment. My mouth lost the horrible sulfurous taste—uremia is the medical term for the condition, which I'd learned from reading When Your Kidneys Fail. I also read that uremia, along with decreased appetite, and feeling cold and tired (symptoms of anemia), are important symptoms of kidney failure, all of which I'd experienced but had failed to understand.

When I finally made it back to my room, the fact that my hospital breakfast had sat waiting for over three hours did nothing to assuage my hunger. I slathered the stale bagel with cream cheese and tore into the two cold hard-boiled eggs. It was one of the most delicious breakfasts I've ever eaten.

The hunger I felt and the satiation I experienced afterward reminded me of what it felt to be healthy again. I felt a whisper of hope. I wasn't dead, yet. Technology was giving me a second chance.

The rest of Wednesday passed in a blur of meaningless cable TV shows, until ABC News interrupted General Hospital with live coverage of President Clinton's decision to bomb Baghdad. I promptly turned off the TV. With the current events in my own life, Iraq really did feel like the other side of the world.

That night I accepted the sleeping pill the nurse offered me. The night before, I'd resolutely refused the pill in what had probably been a subconscious attempt to exert some kind of control, puny though it may have been, over my situation. Now, I lay back on the hospital bed, a quiescent patient, and downed the sleeping pill with a small sip of water. I enjoyed a good night's rest, despite the threat of the upcoming biopsy.

The Biopsy

On Thursday morning, an orderly wheeled me off before breakfast for the kidney biopsy. By now, any residual feelings I might have had about controlling my destiny had evaporated. I passively complied with the myriad instructions, pain notwithstanding.
The most difficult part of the biopsy was having to lie absolutely motionless on my stomach on a large mechanized

tray with my neck twisted hard to the side, while the tray slid me back and forth through the center of the massive cylindrical MRI machine. A grating, mechanical-sounding voice told me to "Breathe…Hold your breath…Breathe," on and off for so long I lost track, as they moved me back and forth to zero in on the part of my left kidney they wanted to extract.

Fortunately, I hardly felt the three biopsies they took, because the pain in my neck had grown to such a degree that all I could think about was when it would be over and I'd be able to unkink my neck. Fortunate, how you can't feel more than one excruciating pain at a time. Nature can be merciful on occasion.

My parents arrived late that afternoon from New Hampshire. They'd left the urban turbulence of LA a few years earlier for the bucolic quiet of New Hampshire, where my mom now taught Electrical Engineering at Dartmouth.

"My poor baby. I wish we could have gotten here sooner." She sat on the bed and hugged me.

Usually an energetic, take-charge sort of person, at the moment, she simply clung to me. Bob stood beside us, quietly supportive.

I felt awkward, unused to being smothered in sympathy, but I also knew how difficult it must be for them to see me and not be able to do anything. On Monday when I was first hospitalized I'd hated this feeling of powerlessness, but now, four days later, I'd begun to grow accustomed to it. They were still new to the experience.

"I'll order take-out from the Mediterranean deli." Marla took charge and orchestrated dinner for everyone else.

That night, while they dined on delicious mezzas, I picked at the "renal-friendly" hospital faire: limp broccoli, tasteless, cold mashed potatoes, thin gravy and some kind of bland white meat, possibly pork.

The biopsy results were due back the next day and would tell us whether or not my kidney failure was reversible. As Dr. Pali had said, there was a possibility that I had acute nephritis, a reversible condition in which the kidneys suddenly shut down but then just as suddenly resume functioning again. That's what we were all hoping for.

Friday morning, Kurt left for work, Marla was off at a job interview, and my parents came and kept me company while we waited. And waited. The clock ticked.

We took a walk around the hospital and discovered the chapel on the first floor. It was a small, windowless room, but one end of it consisted of an illuminated, stained glass picture, an abstract image of a yellow sun on the horizon of a blue ocean bordered by green hills and trees. We sat on several of the benches in the quiet room.

"Let's pray," Mom said.

Her suggestion surprised me. Though she'd been raised Protestant and Bob Church of England, they both had been Unitarian Universalists as long as they'd been together.

Growing up with them as a UU, I'd always thought myself the maker of my world, and I took both responsibility and credit for my life. Prayer had never been something I practiced. I'd rarely anthropomorphized the greater power referred to in Christianity as God.

But now, as I sat there looking at the peaceful, abstract image, I wanted to pray. I wanted to believe God was an understanding father figure, a kind and loving parent. I longed to have the faith I'd seen in others, like Kayla, like my father's relatives who, as devout evangelical Christians, never seemed to feel alone, abandoned, or forsaken. If only, if only there could be the chance of reversibility... I prayed.

Our wait continued until late afternoon, when Mom ran out of patience. She flagged down a nurse to find the doctor. Within half an hour, Dr. Pali hurried into the hospital room. Her face was grim as I introduced her to my parents.

"Nice to meet you," she said as she sat down on the one free chair. "I have been struggling all afternoon with how to tell you the unfortunate news. I'd hoped that with such a sudden onset of your symptoms that your diagnosis would be acute nephritis. Unfortunately, however, that's not the case.

The biopsy revealed that only four percent of your kidneys remain functional."

Her words came to me through an obscure haze, as though I heard them from a vast distance and could only barely register their meaning. Mom interrupted Dr. Pali, having adapted since yesterday to the idea of her daughter as patient.

"Four percent sounds bad, but it doesn't sound like complete kidney failure." Hope laced her voice.

Dr. Pali wasn't put off by the question and replied with great earnestness.

"Until kidney function falls below twenty percent, people do not typically experience symptoms of kidney failure. In Lisa's case, the biopsy showed very few of her nephrons have any filtering capacity left, and even in those instances, the nephrons appear compromised."

Dr. Pali turned to me, her expression sad.

"I really don't know how else to tell you this, Lisa, but you have end stage renal disease. My preliminary diagnosis is diffuse crescentic glomerulonephritis. We have sent a specimen to the specialists at UCSF for further analysis. We should know by next week what the underlying pathology is."

After Dr. Pali left, our mood was dark, and my last night in the hospital was not pleasant. Any hope of reversal had disappeared. The future looked bleak. While my family sat beside me in the hospital room eating Italian deli, I reclined despondently in bed. Depressed and running a low-grade fever, I wasn't hungry.

I'd been in survival mode during most of my hospital stay, focused solely on making it through each day and each procedure without accessing any deep emotion. It all had a feeling of unreality to it, as though it were happening to someone else. I felt like I was living in a bad, made-for-TV melodrama: the successful young career woman with her loving husband and family is suddenly struck down by some inexplicable disease—the shock, the horror. But this movie didn't end with the clean, smooth finality of a mortal tragedy. I wasn't dead, but I wasn't "cured," either.

After my family left for the night, I touched the permacatheter tubes hanging from my chest and thought about leaving the hospital. My life had fallen apart outside these walls and the idea of leaving frightened me. Though my experience in the hospital hadn't been great, I'd come to feel safe here. They'd brought me food, taken me to dialysis, and left me alone in my room to rest most of the time. Nothing was required of me except to follow their orders. Leaving this security would mean having to fend for myself in the world again. I'd have to go to an outpatient hemodialysis clinic three times a week on my own, and I'd have to go back to work. Realizing how profoundly my life was about to change, I was terrified.

Chapter 3 - Hemodialysis

The Hemodialysis Clinic

I left the hospital the weekend before Christmas, with two dead kidneys and two tubes sticking out of my chest. With the holiday season gearing up, Helen and I agreed that I didn't need to go back to work until after New Years. I'd also accrued enough vacation time to still get paid for my time off. The Tuesday after getting out of the hospital, I had my first outpatient hemodialysis treatment.

It was one of those surprisingly warm, sunny days that sometimes grace the Bay Area in late December. Mom offered to take me to the dialysis clinic, since Kurt had to work and Marla and Bob needed to go holiday shopping.

The clinic was located across Berkeley in the more congested south side of town and parking was a hassle. We eventually found a metered spot a few blocks from the clinic. I got out of the car and read the small print on the parking meter.

"This is only good for two hours! My dialysis is going to run a lot longer than that. What am I going to do after the holidays, when you and Bob are gone and I have to start driving myself here?" I was stressed out enough about my first trip to the outpatient clinic. "I'll have to get a handicap placard, but when on earth will I have time to go to the DMV and stand in those long lines?" I felt my tension level rise.

"Maybe Marla can go. She hasn't landed a job yet."

"I guess that'll work, but I hope she doesn't mind going for me." I didn't like bothering other people with my problems. Having to ask Marla for help just added to my feeling stressed out.

"I'll make sure and put some more money in the meter after two hours," Mom said as we headed inside.

The clinic's small waiting room was crowded. We'd arrived half an hour early as instructed to allow enough time to check in with Gabrielle, the administrative assistant, and give the nurses enough time to prep one of the dialysis machines for my 2 p.m. scheduled hook up.

I filled out the paperwork, trying to keep a tight reign on my emotions, but my control slipped. I glanced around the room and noticed the other patients, especially those who looked ill, and I smelled the distinct, off-putting odors of the place. I began to feel sorry for myself. Despite my efforts to appear courageous and restrain my emotions in front of so many people also undergoing hardship, I started to cry.

Gabrielle came to my rescue by asking me a lot of questions about the paperwork and why I had kidney failure.

As I answered her, I tried not to notice how strange she looked. Her eyes protruded, her face had a balloon-like roundness, and her body was massively swollen, bulging through her black jeans and sweater. Despite her physical problems, she was incredibly cheerful. Without preamble, she told me about her own experience with disease.

"The cancer wasn't something they could operate on, so they dosed me up on prednisone to try and stop it. That's why I look like this." She gestured bluntly but without anger at her body. "They've got me on so much prednisone I'm surprised I don't pop!" She laughed. "But I can't complain. It ain't so bad, and it sure beats being dead, don't it!" Her bright smile lit up her dark moon face.

I couldn't understand how Gabrielle could be so happy and hopeful while at the same time battling for her life. The somber, frail, hopeless-looking countenances of several of the waiting dialysis patients made much more sense to me. Nevertheless, Gabrielle's cheerful words helped slow my tears.

I finished speaking with her and sat down next to Mom. The loud TV, possibly turned up for the hearing-impaired patients, inhibited conversation, so we waited in silence.

Shortly before 2 p.m., one of the dialysis assistants, a slim Filipino man with spiky hair and a gold hoop in his left ear, poked his head through the door dividing the waiting room from the clinic.

"Lisa? We're ready to weigh you." He held the door open for us.

We entered the dialysis room. I assiduously avoided looking around, afraid to see what awaited me. Instead, I stared down at the scale. Adjacent to the door and next to the wall, it was a large, depressible metal plank built into the floor. The digital readout was attached to the wall at eye level.

"It's built that way for people in wheelchairs," the nurse explained. "Go ahead and step onto it. There you go. You're sixty-five kilograms today."

I couldn't remember the conversion. Mom piped up. "That's one hundred and forty-five pounds, right?"

"Yeah. Maybe a little less, but we do everything in metric. Lisa, do you know what your dry weight is?" the assistant asked.

I didn't know what he was talking about.

"How much do you weigh before dialysis, before you put on fluid?"

I'd stopped peeing as soon as they put me on dialysis, which meant that any fluids I drank had no way of leaving my body on their own, but I couldn't remember if I'd been weighed while in the hospital.

"I think I weighed about a hundred and forty before I was hospitalized." I couldn't remember, so I guessed.

"We can work with that," he said. "Let's assume you've put on two kilos since your last dialysis, so our goal today will be to get you down to sixty-three kilograms." He wrote this information in my chart.

Near the entrance stood a large workstation where several nurses bent over open charts. As we approached, a woman seated behind a computer at one end of the workstation stopped us. She wasn't dressed like a nurse but as an administrator, in a beige, businesslike outfit.

"Excuse me, but only patients are allowed in the dialysis area." She pointedly addressed Mom.

"This is my daughter's first time here. I want to make sure she is well taken care of," Mom said, standing her ground.

At six feet and two inches tall, Mom towered over the woman sitting at the computer. The administrator rose to her feet. She was both tall and large. She took off her reading glasses.

"Of course, but we need to keep the clinic orderly and sanitary, so it's our policy to limit visitors to the waiting area."

When Mom started to object, I interrupted, embarrassed by the fuss being made over me and not wanting to cause ill will in the people upon whom my life was about to depend.

"It's OK, Mom. Let's find out when I'll be done so you can come back and get me." I turned to the administrator. "Do you know how long my dialysis will take?"

"Four hours. Our clinic closes at six o'clock." She sat back down at her computer.

Once Mom left, I turned around and finally faced the dialysis floor. Thirty or so patients reclined in large, adjustable hospital chairs listlessly watching the TVs bolted to the ceiling above each of their dialysis stations. Tubes ran from their bodies to the machines and back, their blood flowing out and then back into them. Nurses fluttered about the room. The air was cluttered with the cacophony of the different cable network shows, the piped-in Christmas Musak, the sporadic beeping alarms of dialysis machines needing adjustment, and the combined odors of alcohol, vinegar, and that other indefinable, ominous smell I was beginning to recognize.

Overwhelmed, I again lost control and began to cry. A huge nurse hulked over.

"Poor dear, I'm Natalie. I'm gonna be your nurse for today. Poor honey." She led me to the waiting dialysis chair.

At first I thought Natalie looked ridiculous. She was enormously fat, but surprisingly light on her feet. Although she had to wear the standard-issue, blue paper surgery covers over her shoes and over her wildly puffy, red-dyed brown hair, her nurse's outfit was bright magenta, and she wore electric blue eye shadow and ruby lipstick. As she settled me in the chair and offered me a tissue, she spoke in a high-pitched, lispy voice that held just a trace of a Latino accent.

DIALYSIS: A MEMOIR

"Honey, why you crying? You don't need to cry. Honey, you're beautiful."

She brushed the hair from my face and handed me a paper face mask while she pulled hers up over her mouth. I noticed her brightly painted fingernails had little Christmas trees on her left index and right ring fingers.

"I like your fingernails." I hoped the words would convey my thanks for her emotional support.

"Aren't they fun?" Her kind brown eyes smiled above the mask.

She pulled on latex gloves and undid the tape on my permacatheter leads, first from the red and then from the blue valves. She snapped off the valve ends and deftly hooked me up to the dialysis machine.

I watched in fascinated horror as my blood left my body and flowed toward the machine. I felt the cool flow of the saline into my body and the corresponding chill flood through me. The sight and sensations were still new. Whereas dialysis in the hospital had felt like a special procedure, here it threatened the possibility of a lifetime. The tears welled up again.

Natalie didn't miss a thing. As she finished recording my vital signs, she distracted me from my dark thoughts by telling me her life story. At twenty-eight, she developed breast cancer and subsequently lost a breast, but she also had the good fortune of bearing seven sons and, at fifty-three, she felt incredibly lucky to be alive. She held a deep and abiding belief in the power of faith.

"Honey, if you pray and if God grants you mercy, you can live." She spoke with earnest sincerity.

She felt her work as a dialysis nurse served a divine purpose. After fifteen years in the profession, she continued to believe that God kept her healthy and cancer-free so that she could continue to help dialysis patients.

Once I was hooked up, she helped me push my chair back into a semi-reclining position and handed me the remote for the TV hanging above my chair.

For the first hour or so, I felt nothing more than a mild chill. Though the dialysis machine warmed the blood as it traveled through the artificial kidney, it inevitably cooled in the tube on its way back to me, and I grew colder as the hours continued. Like many of the other patients, I huddled under one of the clinic's blue polyester blankets, which wasn't long enough to cover my feet. I vowed to bring a jacket and wool socks next time.

Bored watching TV, I looked around the dialysis floor. Each nurse worked a set of chairs and, as I was to learn, some of the nurses were friendlier than others. I watched the nurse attending the patients directly to my left. In contrast to Natalie's gregarious and sometimes comic personality, Delia was the model of efficiency. Middle-aged, she was petite, her hair short and sleek under her paper cap. She didn't mince words as she focused professionally on the task at hand, smacking her gum while she worked. I appreciated her no-nonsense attitude. Later, I'd come to hope she'd be my nurse each dialysis day. Her efficient care typically meant I was hooked up and unhooked promptly, without all the time taken by the drama of Natalie's approach or the bungling ineptitude of some of the other nurses.

Not everyone liked Delia's professionalism. As I watched her move expertly about her job, one of her patients grew irritated by her efficient style. Leon was an older, sharply dressed man, who wore perfectly shined, patent leather shoes and fancy argyle socks, which showed prominently as he reclined in his chair. Rather than sleep or watch TV like the other patients, he preferred to talk. He especially enjoyed flirting with the female nurses. He sat two chairs over from me and heckled Delia.

"I like all them Filipino dishes, except that chicken dish. What's it called?"

"Adobo?" Delia asked as she hooked up Maisie, the patient beside Leon.

"Yeah, that's the one."

"My husband doesn't like adobo," Delia said.

"If I was your husband," Leon grinned suggestively at her, "I wouldn't let you eat that stuff, either!"

When Delia didn't react to his flirtatious comment but kept her attention on the patient beside him, Leon grew agitated.

"Do I gotta have these hoses running across me?" He shouted, not completely joking as he tugged on his blood lines. "They make me feel violated!"

Hearing the commotion, Natalie rushed over to soothe his feelings.

"You wanna rum cake, Honey? I'm gonna give you some sugar. I'll give you a kiss." She leaned her bulk over him and prepared to kiss him on the forehead.

Leon turned his head aside, chuckling. "I'll take the rum cake." They both laughed, and his good humor was restored.

Maisie reclined in her chair between Leon and me, acting depressed. Her clothes were ratty and the soles of her running shoes were worn out. She'd missed her previous dialysis session and had put on eight kilograms (seventeen pounds!) of fluid. Delia had lectured her about the necessity of taking responsibility for her healthcare, but she seemed despondent.

During the course of our dialysis session, she kept muttering to herself, "I ain't got nothin'."

While Leon flirted with Delia and then joked with Natalie, Maisie's muttering grew louder. Later, when Leon was eating a sandwich, she burst out with a loud mutter, "I don't git nothin'."

Leon leaned over and said, "Well, you could git some of my sandwich."

Maisie sulked, her head against her chest, and didn't respond. Leon flagged down Delia, who handed half the sandwich to Maisie.

"Here you go, Maisie. Leon wants you to have this."

Maisie didn't say anything, but she did take the sandwich. She slowly chewed it.

During a later dialysis session, she brought in a bag of McDonald's and obstinately ate a cheeseburger, despite having to endure a lengthy harangue by the staff for eating forbidden foods. Salt is a huge no-no for dialysis patients because it causes fluid retention and inhibits dialysis from working correctly, and American cheese is loaded with phosphorus, which causes calcium to leech from the bones of dialysis patients. Maisie didn't seem to care.

I didn't want to end up hopeless like Maisie, and I especially didn't want to end up like Mr. Simons, another patient on my shift. He epitomized the nightmare vision of a life long spent on dialysis. He needed a personal attendant to escort him in his wheelchair to and from the clinic. His skin had the peculiar appearance that many white people who've been on dialysis a long time seem to develop. It had lost the pink, plump fleshiness of health, fading to a dried out yellowish color, and seemed merely a paper-like covering to the skeleton beneath. On his scalp where the scanty hair failed to hide it, the skin hung in whitish clumps of dandruff and decay. The whites of his eyes had long since bleared to a rheumy yellow.

Dialysis removes many but not all of the toxins in one's body, and it was as if all the years Mr. Simons had been on dialysis were finally catching up with him, the poisons in his body slowly filling him up to his eyeballs. He didn't seem to have much time—or space—left. I don't know what condition led to his kidney failure, but he also had what might have been a colostomy bag connected to his body by a tube. It sat on a little platform underneath the wheelchair, filled with a dark liquid.

He spoke only to answer questions from the nurses, and his responses were slow and low, as though his brain, like his body, had lost its vigor. Most of the time he sat in silence, his head resting on his chest, his eyes half-closed. I watched him sleeping in the dialysis chair directly across from me. He seemed barely alive.

During the final hour on dialysis, my woozy, tearful state gave way to an absurd, hysterical vision. The clinic no longer seemed monstrous to me, but hilariously funny. I found myself imagining the clinic as a ridiculous musical like Rocky Horror Picture Show, but instead of dinner guests dancing in a prelude to eating Eddie, I envisioned the nurses and patients all dancing, white sterile outfits and blood lines entangling, to the swelling strains of Christmas Musak. Natalie starred as a cross between Dr. Frank N. Furter and Magenta.

Then the vision cleared. The positive energy and humor of the interchanges between Natalie, Delia, and Leon reassured me of the basic humanity of the place, and the clinic began to feel like a real community that connected people with one another. I was a part of it through my dependence on the nurses and the life-giving machines. Instead of horror, I started to feel both gratitude and respect.

That first day at the clinic went like clockwork. When Mom poked her head into the dialysis room at 5:55 p.m., Natalie was in the process of unhooking me.

"That wasn't so bad, honey, was it?" Natalie pushed my chair forward into a sitting position and helped me to my feet. She didn't let go of my arm, which was a good thing, because I wobbled when I stood.

"No, it wasn't so bad. Thanks. I'm OK, now."

I moved away from Natalie and toward Mom, who waited by the door. I still felt woozy and very weak, but I didn't want Natalie making a fuss over me, so I forced myself to cross the room as smoothly as possible.

"Hey, Lisa." The male nurse who'd weighed me earlier came over. "Before you go, just step onto the scales here. We've gotta get your weight again. Excellent! You're down to sixty-three kilos, right on target."

He called the numbers out to Natalie, who added them to the other details she was recording in my chart.

"See you next time." He gave a little wave as we left.

Rush hour across Berkeley doubled our travel time home, and what would have been a ten-minute drive took twenty. After an initial exclamation of frustration at the traffic snarl, Mom shrugged and turned to me.

"So, how did it go? What did you do for the four hours? Were you bored?" She wasn't someone who could sit still for any length of time.

I lay my head back against the passenger seat. I felt tired, cold, and wrung out.

"It wasn't so bad. I watched some TV. The dialysis made me hungry at first, but then I got cold and really sleepy."

"I bet you could get a lot done during those four hours. You can probably work out a deal with Helen so you can maintain your billing hours. Have you thought about a cell phone? I could call you and keep you company once I get back to Hanover. I'll have Bob look into it."

I hadn't thought about how I'd integrate dialysis into my work schedule. I knew I'd stress out about all that soon enough. At the moment, I felt too tired to think about it. I closed my eyes.

"Sure, a cell phone sounds like a good idea. What are Marla and Bob making for dinner?" I changed the subject, still feeling slightly hungry.

After dinner, I lay on the couch and thought about the clinic and the different attitudes of the people there. In contrast to Maisie and Mr. Simons, Gabrielle, Natalie, and Leon managed to maintain positive outlooks. Their optimistic attitudes uplifted the people around them. I wanted to be like them. I didn't want to end up like Mr. Simons, and I was determined to prevent myself from falling into the despondency that infected Maisie.

The Blood Transfusion

During my hospital stay, Dr. Pali had explained that kidney failure meant my kidneys no longer produced the hormone erythropoietin, which tells the bone marrow to create new red blood cells. She recommended a transfusion and told me that a fresh infusion of blood would return energy and warmth to my body.

DIALYSIS: A MEMOIR

At the time, I'd felt unable to contemplate one more hospital procedure, so I'd refused. Receiving someone else's blood frightened me, and I was still trying to make peace with dialysis and the idea of having my blood flow out of my body and through a machine. During the first week home from the hospital, however, I found the anemia increasingly distressing.

While giving myself my first sponge bath (the permacatheter prohibited showering), I stood shivering and stared at my feet on the cold tile of the bathroom floor. They didn't seem like my feet. They reminded me of a corpse I'd once seen on a high school field trip to UCLA medical school. I experienced a similar sense of disconnect—to know that what I was looking at was like me—in this case, was me—and yet my feet looked so alien, so different. My shriveled white feet looked more like those of that corpse than my own.

This experience, combined with an exhaustion and weakness that left me unable to do much more than huddle under a pile of blankets on the couch, convinced me that a blood transfusion might help give me back some of my former energy.

On December 23, Mom and Marla drove me to the outpatient hemapheresis center first thing in the morning. They planned to return in an hour after some last-minute Christmas shopping, and I hadn't wanted the stress and drama of their staying with me through the procedure. We assumed blood transfusions were as simple as donating blood, just in reverse.

"Oh no, not an hour." The nurse contradicted our assumption. "It will take at least three hours, but probably more like four, for Lisa to receive two units of blood."

When she saw our shocked expressions, she explained.

"Transfusing blood is nothing like donating. We have to be careful that Lisa's body accepts the new blood without any rejection problems, so we have to do it slowly and give her body time to adjust."

She turned to me. "We'll monitor you very closely to make sure your body accepts the new blood."

Her words only minimally reduced the fear I had of receiving a stranger's blood.

"Are you going to be OK? You sure you don't want us to stay?" Marla asked.

"I'll be fine. It's not any longer than my dialysis time was yesterday. Besides, I've got a book to read. Go shopping and have a good time. I'll see you when you get back."

Unlike the crowded and bustling dialysis clinic, the plasma center housed only six beds. Besides one other patient who lay quietly receiving her blood and the two nurses who periodically checked on us, I was left alone. There were no TVs, no weird smells, and no drama, except for the plot of the mindless suspense novel lent me by a co-worker. I read for a while as I reclined on the bed receiving the blood, but then I set the book down on my lap.

I looked up at the bag of blood hanging from the IV pole, feeling the drop-by-drop cool flow of someone else's blood entering my body. The sensation was not unpleasant, though the blood lost some warmth as it traveled down the tube from the bag. I wondered about the donors who'd taken time out to donate during the busy holiday season.

At first, I felt fear. What undetected diseases, perhaps even more hideous than HIV or hepatitis C, might the blood harbor? What unforeseen new danger did I risk by receiving a stranger's blood? But then, as I felt the welcome warmth seep into my bones, the fear melted into a profound sense of gratitude. I sent a heartfelt silent thanks to the two anonymous donors who'd sacrificed their time and blood to selflessly help others in need.

When Marla and Mom finally returned to pick me up, they exclaimed how "pink" I looked. As I walked out to the car and felt the distant winter sun on my face, I felt stronger and warmer than I had in months.

The Diagnosis

DIALYSIS: A MEMOIR

Dr. Pali called at lunchtime on Christmas Eve with the results of my biopsy. We were all there, Kurt, Marla, my parents, and Bob's son, Liam, who'd just arrived for a holiday visit. I put the doctor on speaker and we all gathered about the phone to hear what she had to say.

"The results have finally arrived from the specialists at UCSF." She spoke hurriedly. "The results are conclusive. Unfortunately, you have a rare autoimmune disease known as anti-glomerular basement membrane disease."

"Anti-glom—what?" I asked, unable to decipher the unfamiliar words made more obscure by her accent.

Mom grabbed a pen and paper. "Can you spell that?" She wrote down the letters Dr. Pali enunciated.

We stood stunned by the phone as Dr. Pali rushed on.

"Your body generated anti-GBM antibodies that attacked the glomerular basement membrane lining the nephrons of your kidneys. Your nephrons are supposed to filter your blood, but the anti-GBM antibodies caused such extensive scarring that they no longer work. The good news is that since we have a positive diagnosis for why your kidneys failed, we can now monitor the status of your disease by measuring your anti-GBM antibody levels. We should have an antibody count back from the lab shortly. I'll call you when the results are in."

Her words washed meaninglessly over me. I hung up the phone, still trying to pronounce the diagnosis. Everyone else broke into speech. Liam hadn't known the details of my hospitalization and wanted a recap of events. Bob and Marla filled him in while Mom discussed with Kurt how to find out more about the disease. I sat silently at the dining room table, aware of the permacath dangling stiff and alien from my chest under my sweater, and pondered the fact that I had an autoimmune disease that had irrevocably destroyed a part of myself.

Normal diseases, where some outside force threatens the body, made sense to me, and I'd conquered the six-month stint of hyperthyroidism I'd experienced three years earlier (or so I believed) by taking control of myself and changing my mental outlook. This "anti-GBM" seemed too extreme, too destructive. How could my own body have done this to me? I felt powerless in the face of such vast devastation.

Mom, an adept research academic, went online to dig up as much information as she could and, several days later, handed me the pile of web pages she'd printed out.

"It turns that in addition to the nephrons of your kidneys, glomerular basement membranes also line the alveoli of your lungs. Thank goodness you never smoked! If you had, the antibodies could have attacked your lungs. That's a disease called Goodpasture's Syndrome. It's more common and much deadlier than what you have." She liked to keep worst-case scenarios in mind; they helped her feel better about reality.

I lay on the couch and thumbed through the printouts. Her research left me puzzled about why I'd developed such a rare disease but thankful that it hadn't attacked my lungs. Kidney failure was nothing like lung failure. Dialysis would keep me alive, at least until I could obtain a transplant.

But why did I get anti-GBM? Like all autoimmune diseases, there had to be a genetic component, but no one in my family (as far as I know) had ever had this disease or died of kidney failure. I wondered if something I did was responsible, like all the years of drinking too much. Superstitiously, I remembered once consulting a palm reading book in high school and noticing the short life line on my left hand. Had I been doomed from the start?

In her research, Mom uncovered an epidemiological study suggesting a link between hydrocarbon exposure and anti-GBM disease. The study revealed a slightly higher prevalence of anti-GBM in young male auto mechanics. Looking for personal correlations, I recalled the years I spent training on my bike in the hydrocarbon-filled air of LA as well as my childhood growing up in the seventies in the San Gabriel Valley, one of the smoggiest places in the United States at the time. I also thought about those six months of hyperthyroidism and wondered if some underlying phenomenon was leading my body to attack itself.

DIALYSIS: A MEMOIR

As I lay on the couch, I imagined the anti-GBM antibodies coursing through my blood. How could my body destroy itself? Why? It seemed inexplicable. I watched Mom sitting on her side of the couch poring over a stack of scientific articles. Acquiring knowledge helped her feel better; it gave her some intellectual control over the situation. I, however, felt unable to face the facts of my disease. Knowledge wouldn't change the situation and cure my dead kidneys. I put the pile of articles and abstracts on the floor and slipped into sleep.

When I didn't hear from Dr. Pali in the week after Christmas, I impatiently called her office, knowing the lab results must be back. The anti-GBM antibody count would determine the timing of the transplant, and I was anxious to know what the future would hold. She didn't return my calls, which left me with a feeling I was only just coming to know, a contradictory combination of angry frustrated powerlessness and helpless dependence, at the whim and mercy of someone else's priorities.

Dr. Pali finally delivered the fateful news during her clinic rounds on Saturday. She baldly conveyed the information as I lay helpless in the dialysis chair, tied to the dialysis machine by my blood lines.

"Your anti-GBM antibody titer is four hundred and sixty-six. The normal range is zero. You will need to remain on dialysis until your value decreases to zero. In the meantime, you should meet with the transplant doctors to discuss the transplant options."

Speechless, my mind reeled with this new information. Four hundred and sixty-six seemed so high. When I finally thought to ask Dr. Pali exactly how long it might take for my antibodies to decrease to zero, she had already moved on to her next patient. I spent the rest of the day's dialysis hoping it wouldn't take too long for the antibodies to go away.

The Transplant Clinic

The meeting with the transplant doctor took place the first week of January. Located at the top floor of a six-story office building, the transplant office looked like a place for commercial business and for selling the image of its transplant group as highly successful, nothing like the dialysis clinic or the hospital, both several blocks away and shaggy around the edges, rundown from heavy use.

My whole family waited in the comfortable reception room, the pale blue décor trimmed in gold. We were there as a united front, ready to face the future when the transplant would become a reality.

Bob had blood type AB-negative, known as "universal recipient," and could receive blood from anyone, but he could only donate to other people with AB-negative blood. This meant he couldn't donate a kidney to me. Mom, who was type O or "universal donor," could possibly donate, and Marla, who had my same blood type, A-positive, would probably be the best candidate.

Kurt had an extreme blood phobia, so I was surprised to find that he had gone to get his blood typed while I was still in the hospital. I'd been too sick at the time to fully appreciate what this must have been like for him, to overcome his fear of blood and needles in order to get tested. His blood phobia was so extreme that he fled his one and only visit to the hemodialysis clinic in horror. As it was, the blood test revealed he was type O and, like Marla and Mom, also qualified as a potential donor.

The visit with the transplant doctor did not begin well. While the transplant coordinator gave us the sales pitch for the transplant group and touted its high success rate compared to national averages, a man hurried into the room and interrupted her.

"Where are those files?" He didn't make eye contact or acknowledge any of us.

The coordinator leapt to her feet and accompanied him out of the room.

"How rude," Bob said.

DIALYSIS: A MEMOIR

"I'll bet he's Dr. Brass," Mom said. "One of those rude, know-it-all type doctors."

Kurt and I didn't respond, though Marla, who disliked contention, hissed "Mom!" in disapproval.

Matters didn't improve when we were kept waiting for almost an hour. The tension built. Marla, Kurt and I made small talk about Marla's upcoming return visit to Hawaii for her birthday, while Bob thumbed through some of the magazines and Mom jotted down notes and questions from the latest stack of medical articles she'd printed from the Internet in preparation for the meeting.

When Dr. Brass finally returned, the coordinator performed introductions and emphasized his importance as the head of the transplant team. Dr. Brass immediately whisked me off for a cursory physical exam. He was in his mid-to-late-sixties, with a thick thatch of gray-white hair and a bulging belly only partly disguised by the brown tweed coat and wide tie. He belonged to the "old school" of authority and reminded me of an old Harvard professor I'd once taken a course from, a man who smiled a little smugly and looked slightly askance when confronted by what he dismissed as the naïve ignorance of those beneath him, particularly young women like me.

I thought our meeting was supposed to be introductory, so the reason for the physical exam seemed unclear. I was sure he must have already seen my chart, which included all the data he was obtaining in the exam and which was updated weekly at the dialysis clinic. As he pumped up the blood pressure cuff, I asked him about the timing of the transplant, but rather than look at me, he addressed the new chart he was generating.

"All in good time, my dear, all in good time." He nodded sagely and wrote down my blood pressure values.

The meaning behind his words was clear: I was to play by his rules, his schedule, because he knew what was best for me. I sat on the examining table with my hands limp in my lap, once again experiencing the unpleasant sensation of being both powerless and dependent.

After the exam, he escorted me into another room where my family sat waiting for us around a large circular table. The meeting room had a wide picture window facing north over town and toward the Berkeley hills. The day was sunny though a bit hazy.

Dr. Brass leaned back in his chair and opened the thin chart. It struck me as strange that he didn't have my real chart, the one that had grown as thick as a telephone book. He peered over the rim of the glasses perched on his nose and began interviewing each of us. He asked about our jobs, our hobbies, our relationships with each other, and jotted brief notes in the chart. I assumed this was to determine if, based on our emotional and financial support networks, we'd be good candidates for a transplant. He then eased back in his chair and steepled his fingertips across his chest.

"Well," he said, looking at each of us with a broad smile, "I don't see any reason why we can't go ahead and schedule Lisa for a transplant right away."

"What?!" Mom exclaimed. "She has anti-GBM! She has to wait at least six months after her antibodies have disappeared before she can have a transplant. Otherwise, the donated kidney will be at risk." She leaned forward across the table toward Dr. Brass, outrage and disbelief coloring her voice.

"Where did you hear such a thing?" Dr. Brass looked down at the chart in his hands, not meeting her gaze.

"I've spent a great deal of time researching my daughter's illness, and I've read most of the current articles available on the Internet."

"Ah, the Internet." Dr. Brass raised his shaggy eyebrows and looked up from the chart. "You know you can't trust everything you read on the Internet."

This was too much for Mom, who said with pride, "There are three PhD's sitting around this table, Doctor, and we know how to discern fact from fiction."

I could tell that she saw in him the same kind of "old school" male authority figure I had, but her reaction was exacerbated by the fact that she'd spent an entire career in the hard sciences competing against men like this.

I swallowed and surreptitiously glanced around the table. Bob and Kurt looked mildly uncomfortable at the direction the conversation was heading, but Marla's eyes met mine, distressed. She hated Mom's aggressive competitiveness, and as sister, we immediately recognized the combative tone in her voice.

Refusing to acknowledge Mom's comment, Dr. Brass cleared his throat and issued his response with cool, paternal authority. A slight sneer curved his lips.

"I am an MD." He emphasized the degree and looked around the table at each of us. "I'm the head of the transplant team, which consists of ten superlative nephrologists. As an MD, there are things I know that a PhD would not. I'm sure you know that my team is nationally recognized as one of the best in the country. We've been successfully transplanting kidneys for over ten years. You do trust that I know my job?"

"Doctor," Marla interjected. "What were the results of the tissue-typing test?"

Unlike my response to the growing animosity between Mom and Dr. Brass—retreating inside myself and perhaps perversely wanting to watch the impending fight—Marla courageously stepped into the fray as peacemaker and tried to divert them.

Her tactic worked. Dr. Brass regained his prior magnanimity as he addressed the details of tissue typing. He explained that each person has six antigens and, while not necessary for donor eligibility, the more the antigens match the better the chances the body will accept the kidney.

Despite not having my complete chart, he did have the results of the tissue typing. Surprisingly, Marla and I had no antigens in common; two of Mom's matched, but most surprising was that Kurt and I had three matching antigens.

When we asked Dr. Brass how rare an occurrence this was, he smiled and said simply, "Think of it as a gift."

LISA FRIEDEN

"I read that non-genetically related kidneys do better in cases of autoimmune disorders," Mom said. "Lisa will probably have less trouble with Kurt's kidney because he's not related to her, isn't that right?"

This information ran counter to the general consensus that genetically related kidney transplants faire best.

"I have not read that the survival rate of the graft," Dr. Brass emphasized the medical term for the transplanted kidney, "is improved by non-related donors in the case of autoimmune conditions."

He brought the interview to an abrupt end and shut down any further questions from Mom by snapping the chart closed and rising to his feet.

"We will need to continue to monitor Lisa's anti-GBM antibodies on a monthly basis. It may take as long as two or three years before she will be eligible for a transplant." He offered no admission or apology of his earlier error about my diagnosis and promptly left the room.

As we walked to the parking lot, there was a general outburst.

"I can't believe that man!" Mom fumed.

"How rude!" Bob exclaimed, his Australian accent strengthened by his indignation.

In the backseat of the car, Kurt put his arm around me and frowned. "He hadn't even read your medical chart!"

As Bob steered the car through the busy south Berkeley traffic, Mom ranted, her voice laced with fear as well as anger.

"I hope to God that he isn't an indication of the kind of care you're going to get. I hope the rest of the transplant team isn't as incompetent!"

She continued to denounce the doctor with relish and finished by saying that when she got home, she was going to look up his credentials to see what school he went to and what, if any, papers he'd written. A graduate from Harvard with a PhD from MIT, she herself had authored many papers and had been elected to the most distinguished national organization in her field, the National Academy of Engineers.

DIALYSIS: A MEMOIR

Unlike the others, however, I felt no outrage. Dr. Brass' final words echoed in my mind and left me disheartened. I found little consolation in fantasizing about how some future transplant might save me. A couple of years seemed an eternity. How was I going to manage dialysis with my job?

Chapter 4 - Work

Work to the Rescue

After the holidays, I went back to work. I craved the routine and mundane activities of my job, anything to distract me from my personal situation. Everyone at the office welcomed me back, surprised I didn't look somehow different now that I was on dialysis. They couldn't see the permacatheter tubes hidden under my blouse.

"You look great! You're not so pale." Cara noticed the effects of the blood transfusion.

It felt good to be in the office again, surrounded by eight women my age who, besides their PR work, had little more stressful to think about than what gifts to buy for weddings or their friends' baby showers.

Sitting at my desk, I heard Kristen on the phone in her office across the hall. Her phone conversations, which used to strike me as vacuous and a waste of billable time, I now found reassuring. When she worried on the phone with her husband about what color wallpaper to hang in their kitchen or when she complained to the tree guy about how he'd shaped one of the trees in her garden, I felt a sense of continuity. Despite the death of my kidneys, the rest of the world hadn't changed. Like a breath of fresh air, work relieved me from dwelling on my health problems.

On Mondays, Wednesdays and Fridays, I could pretend life was almost like before. Tuesdays and Thursdays were another story. On those days, I had to integrate the afternoon dialysis treatments with my job. All my life I'd been strong, independent and in control. I wasn't going to allow circumstances to radically change my life now that I was on dialysis. I planned to continue working full time.

"Are you sure you don't want to cut back your hours?" Helen asked when she reviewed my work schedule.

"No, I can handle it," I insisted. "I can work until 1:15 in the office on Tuesdays and Thursdays, and then I can work the rest of the afternoons while I'm on dialysis. That way, I can keep billing full time."

The Internet boom demanded a lot of PR. I knew Helen needed all the help she could get, and I needed to feel needed. We agreed to give the arrangement a try.

Steak and Donuts

Most of my friends found it both emotionally and logistically difficult to visit me at the clinic, especially since everyone was working full time. Only one friend routinely visited me during my four months on hemodialysis. Mel was a quiet, supportive, and indefatigable man, who, despite being the senior software architect at a start up, took time out of his busy schedule to battle the traffic across the Bay Bridge and visit me at the clinic. To sweeten his lengthy drive, I offered the lure of fresh donuts from the excellent donut shop near the clinic, and I invited him to join us for a steak dinner afterwards.

"Besides," I told him during his first visit to the clinic in January, "steak and donuts make the perfect meal for someone on hemodialysis."

"Why's that?" he laughed.

"Because the steak is high in protein and the donuts are low in phosphorus and potassium."

"What's wrong with too much phosphorus or potassium?" None of my other friends had taken the time to ask such detailed questions about my life on dialysis, and Mel didn't seem put off by the clinic, its machinery, or the other patients.

I summarized the lecture the nutritionist had given me when I was first hospitalized.

"Healthy people can regulate the phosphorus and potassium in their blood, but once your kidneys fail, your body can't do this anymore. If your phosphorus level climbs too high, your body tries to correct the imbalance by leeching calcium from your bones, so you risk osteoporosis."

"That sounds serious. So how do you keep it low?"

"You mean besides eating donuts?" I grinned, trying to lighten the conversation. "I take calcium pills whenever I eat anything, in order to help neutralize the phosphorus in the food."

"Wow, I never realized eating could be so complicated. What's the problem with potassium?"

"A high potassium level can be dangerous, since potassium helps regulate the heart. If you eat too much when your kidneys don't work, your heart will stop and you die."

Mel's eyebrows rose. "OK, so steak doesn't have a lot of phosphorus and potassium, but what about cholesterol? Don't you have to worry about heart disease?"

"No. We dialysis patients aren't expected to live long enough to have to worry about that." I laughed darkly.

We planned to go for donuts as soon as I finished dialysis, which would leave us enough time to drive home and have dinner with Kurt by 8 p.m. But my body didn't behave as scheduled. It had its own plans, which subordinated all others.

Like most dialysis patients, kidney failure had made me hypertensive. Without functional kidneys, my body no longer regulated its blood pressure, but unlike the ninety-five percent of patients whose blood pressure drops during dialysis, mine typically rose. That first night Mel visited wasn't unusual. As soon as I was disconnected, my blood pressure spiked.

"What's going on?" Mel asked when he came in from the waiting room and saw me still seated in the dialysis chair.

"My blood pressure is too high, so they gave me some clonidine." I spoke angrily, resentful that my body wouldn't behave. A short-acting antihypertensive, clonidine usually helped restrain my blood pressure when I took it daily, first thing in the morning and last thing before bed, but this time, it didn't work.

"Can't I leave now?" I asked the nurse a few minutes later.

DIALYSIS: A MEMOIR

"Not until your blood pressure comes down."

I explained the situation to Mel, who in his unique, quiet way, took it all in stride. We sat and waited. And waited. The nurses and assistants finished cleaning the room. All the other patients had been disconnected by 6:15 p.m. and were long gone. The place had fallen quiet, the TVs and dialysis machines now silent.

By 7:15 p.m., my nurse, Mel and I were the only ones left in the place. My blood pressure had barely dropped. The nurse looked at her watch and abruptly said, "You should be OK now." She ushered us out the door. She'd abandoned protocol to go home.

It was too late to get donuts. I apologized to Mel and promised we'd get donuts next time. If I'd felt better, I would've been furious. We'd spent all that time waiting around for nothing. The steak dinner wasn't the same without the fresh donuts, but Mel's being there meant something. Unlike so many of us who were caught up in the busy dot com boom, he took the time to visit me during several of those long, dark January nights on dialysis.

There were other nights like that one, when the nurses grew frustrated because my body wouldn't behave and they had to stay beyond their twelve-hour shifts to deal with me.

There was the time my blood pressure inexplicably plummeted and I was unable to rise from the dialysis chair without fainting. I was happy to have low blood pressure, finally, but the nurse insisted I drink salty broth to raise my blood pressure. She wouldn't let me leave until my blood pressure rose enough to meet clinic protocol. Frustrated, I felt like my body was a spastic yo-yo, refusing to support me or abide by the clinic rules.

Another time, the previous patient was extremely late hooking up, so the nurse cut my dialysis time by an hour and a half, just so he could leave by 6:30 p.m. I could understand why the nurses felt little obligation to stay late on their own time to deal with my difficult case, even if it meant I didn't receive a full course of dialysis. I was too strung out and tired to make demands. Like the nurses, I just wanted to get the hell out of there, drive blearily home, and collapse on the couch.

It wasn't until later that I learned that the outpatient clinic I attended was for-profit. Clinics like it have been spreading across the country and replacing the not-for-profit clinics. They want to make money, so the patient functions not just as the customer but also as the commodity. The clinic receives money for each patient it treats, either from insurance companies or the federal government via Medicare.

At my clinic, part of a national chain of for-profit clinics headquartered in another state, the goal was to maximize the number of patients receiving treatment and minimize the number of working staff. At any given time, there were as many as thirty people receiving treatment, tended by nurses and assistants numbering anywhere from five to eight, who worked shifts that lasted twelve hours, but without overtime pay. Though the nurses did the best they could to care for us, they did talk about how tired and overworked they felt.

Human Guinea Pig

The doctors made their clinic rounds only once a week, but they didn't seem aware of the problems at the clinic and I rarely saw them. Dr. Pali, who headed the clinic, was even less available and always seemed in a rush, spending little time with individual patients. My own schedule was jam packed and left me little room for formal appointments with her at her office. We were both too busy to focus enough of our attention on my care to be proactive. Our efforts to combat my hypertension illustrated the reactive nature of our doctor/patient relationship. It played out like a comedy of errors.

Upon my initial diagnosis of hypertension, Dr. Pali prescribed me Procardia, a commonly prescribed blood pressure medication. Within minutes of taking the drug, however, I developed tachycardia and a splitting headache.

Then, several hours later, an attack of hives sent me to the emergency room. It turned out I was allergic.

The message I left for Dr. Pali resulted in her calling in a different drug to the pharmacy, but Verapamil made my face and tongue swell over the course of the following week, one of the rare side effects of the drug.

More days passed, more telephone calls and voicemails were exchanged, and more prescriptions were filled. Zestril gave me a horrible, dry hacking cough. Hydralazine made my heart race. I had dry heaves on metoprolol. Clonidine and Cozaar seemed to work a little and had side effects no worse than a stuffy nose.

With each new drug, the feeling I was a human guinea pig intensified. It culminated late one Thursday night in mid January, when I sat in the emergency room at 1 a.m., waiting for the results of a chest X-ray. I'd experienced a sudden exacerbation of the chest pains that had been plaguing me, so Kurt and I had rushed to ER, worried about my continuing high blood pressure and the possibility of a heart attack.

I lay on the bed in the examining room, exhausted from my earlier dialysis that day, and tried to ignore the painful squeezing inside the left side of my chest. Kurt sat on a chair beside me, leafing through a magazine. This was our third trip to ER in a week, and we were now accustomed to the routine of waiting several hours for an examining room and then waiting again for the ER doctor to finish with his other cases before he could get to mine.

"I'm glad it's the same doc," I said to Kurt. As with before, the ER doctor was friendly and considerate, even at 1 a.m. and rushing between patients.

"He seems to know what he's doing," Kurt said.

Implicit in his comment was a critique of my own doctors, but I didn't respond to him. Instead, I felt frustrated that my body refused to behave like other people's bodies. I thought of all the medications I'd tried in the last three weeks to control my blood pressure. It seemed like I always ended up being one of the unlucky one percent listed in the adverse events section of each drug's information pamphlet. Why didn't the drugs work for me? The pharmaceutical commercials on TV advertised drugs as magic bullets, but I found in my case they were barely usable.

As January progressed, my anger at being powerless to control my body sank into hopelessness. My blood pressure steadily climbed and I developed an excruciating pain in the side of my neck that interfered with sleep. By the end of the month, I was running a blood pressure of 200/134 and feeling like hell.

Reaching My Limit

At first, I imagined using the four hours on dialysis, three days a week, to accomplish vast amounts of uninterrupted work. I had visions of billing the time for client-related activities: writing press releases, researching client technologies, and reading up on the latest industry news.

I soon discovered, however, that this wouldn't be possible. The first hour on dialysis, I remained alert and able to concentrate, but as the time dragged on and my blood continued to cycle through the dialysis machine, I'd sink into a deeper and deeper stupor. It felt like the Demerol they give you in the hospital after an operation. The woozy sensation wasn't unpleasant. In fact, it had a siren-like seductiveness that I found increasingly hard to resist. After a few weeks, I succumbed and often spent a good portion of my dialysis catching up on much needed sleep, something my high blood pressure and neck pain had made an ordeal at home.

Through the month of January, I struggled to fit hemodialysis into my full time work schedule, but I found over time that my plans were doomed to fail. I was supposed to be hooked up at 2 p.m. sharp and then unhooked at 6 p.m. on Tuesdays, Thursdays and Saturdays, but I discovered this rarely went as planned.

I was the last of three sets of dialysis patients to receive treatment each day, and my hook up time was determined by when the earlier patients hooked up. The earliest set of patients came in from 6 a.m. to 10 a.m. Then the machines needed to be cleaned, the lines disposed of, and the machines prepared for the next patients, whose dialysis time ran from 10 a.m. to 2 p.m. Invariably, patients ran late, or there would be trouble with the machines. I considered switching to dialysis early in the morning, but if I did that, I'd waste the rest of the day, because I was always so exhausted after the treatments.

Delays and endless waiting, and then sitting for four long hours on dialysis, all violated what I valued most: the speed and efficiency that drive successful high tech PR. I had carefully cultivated these attributes in myself, but I couldn't control the clinic and the other patients.

Kurt pressed me to switch doctors and to talk to Helen about cutting back my work hours. It was obvious to us both that Dr. Pali and the nephrology group were overextended and unable to really solve my dialysis-related health problems.

"You're not getting adequate care," he insisted. "And working full time is crazy. You're wiping yourself out."

I knew he was right, but I resisted doing anything. Aside from the fact that I didn't have a lot of bandwidth, what with the hours I was working, my skyrocketing blood pressure, and the yo-yo effects of the dialysis, I still wanted to believe my life had not been significantly altered by kidney failure.

Besides, researching and filling out the requisite paperwork to change doctors and medical groups would require taking time out from either my hectic schedule or from Kurt's twelve-hour work day, not an easy thing to do during the Internet boom when everyone around us was working longer than 40 hours per week. It would also mean fighting against and overcoming my exhaustion. I just didn't have the energy.

By the end of January, however, I knew I had to talk to Helen. I wasn't accomplishing any meaningful work while on dialysis, which meant I was losing eight billable hours a week. Nights after dialysis found me drained and depressed. When not making late night trips to ER with blood pressure problems, I spent evenings lying on the couch, unable to do much more than watch TV and tearfully choke down a tasteless renal diet dinner, salt-less and meat-oriented. When I finally spoke to Helen, she allowed me to reduce my hours; she could afford to be understanding, given the red hot economy.

Despite Helen not having a problem with my working less, it was surprising how defeated I felt admitting my health had impacted my ability to do my job. I felt I'd failed, and I didn't want to feel sorry for myself or have other people feel sorry for me. After my talk with Helen, I stopped working on Tuesday and Thursday mornings before dialysis. Instead, I rested and practiced mindfulness meditation.

Chapter 5 - Meditation

Stress Reduction

By mid-January, a month after being hospitalized, I felt the need to process what was happening to me. I needed someone to talk to, but my family and friends were too close. They had their own emotions to deal with, without being burdened by mine, and I purposely minimized talking about myself at work. High tech PR is a stressful business. Everyone in our office worked hard to maintain its unusually optimistic and cheerful atmosphere. I didn't want to bring them down by talking about my troubles.

The logical conclusion was to seek counseling. My HMO allowed ten visits to an authorized therapist, so I selected one from the list in the provider handbook. I picked one who specialized in treating patients who'd suffered traumatic events, especially HIV diagnoses. I figured end stage renal disease fit the criteria of a permanent, life-threatening diagnosis.

I went several times but found the sessions always ended up with me reciting the latest litany of upsetting events and bodily complaints. Therapy can be helpful for dealing with long term emotional issues, but in my case, talking about my daily hassles with dialysis wasn't giving me tools to emotionally cope with them.

The therapist recommended I sign up for a relaxation course offered by a colleague of hers, a Buddhist practitioner affiliated with one of the local hospitals. She thought the course might offer me useful strategies for dealing with the stress of my current situation. I signed up, and she didn't object when I discontinued therapy a few weeks later.

The ten-week relaxation course was held Wednesday nights in the large basement conference room of the local hospital. I missed the first class when a blood pressure incident sent me to ER. I was late for the second class because I'd hurried home through nasty rush hour to grab a quick dinner before heading back across town to the hospital. Already late for the second class, I then got lost looking for the room in the maze of corridors under the hospital.

When I finally rushed into the room, I found the lights out. Only the dim green lights above the emergency exit doors were illuminated. A man's voice filled the darkness, each word spoken slowly, precisely, with distinct enunciation. I hurried to find a place amidst the people lying on the floor, frustrated that I was late and that I'd missed the beginning of class.

Daniel, the course leader, told us to focus on our breathing and the simple motion of the air flowing into and out of our abdomens, as we practiced what he called the "Body Scan."

Long, long periods of silence followed his instructions. When he did speak, his words came so slowly, so precisely, that I grew irritated and impatient. Why couldn't he speak more quickly? Why wouldn't he hurry up with the next thing we were supposed to focus on?

My mind ran through all the things I needed to do: lists of work-related tasks, chores at home, people I had to call. Lying on the floor doing nothing but breathing seemed pointless. It felt like a complete waste of time.

Other people also had issues with lying still. One woman groaned and complained of an excruciating pain in her neck from having to lie flat on her back. Daniel silently had her shift to sit upright in a chair. Before long, gusty snores emanated from several people in the room.

Finally, he spoke again. His words broke my train of thought and brought me back to my body's presence, lying on the basement floor of the hospital along with fifteen other people, all of us trying to just breathe. He directed us to move our attention to the smallest toe of our left foot and imagine our breath coming in through our lungs and into that toe, filling it with air.

I tried, but I couldn't feel my smallest left toe. As Daniel had us imagine each of our ten toes in succession, I found I couldn't feel any of them. If I could have pressed on my toes with my fingers, or if I could've pushed them against the floor, I knew I would have felt them. Trying to feel my toes from the inside out, in and of themselves, I felt nothing.

Surprised and dismayed, I couldn't remember when I'd last actually experienced the sensation in each toe. Had it really been since my childhood? Or, was this lack of sensation a result of kidney failure?

As long as I could remember, I'd taken the existence of my body for granted. I sensed my body only if something happened to it. I had never experienced it being, in and of itself. My life had always been oriented toward doing, toward action, toward effecting change in the world.

Though I spent the rest of my first Body Scan falling into the soundest sleep I'd had in weeks, the subsequent daily meditation I practiced began to create a space in my mind and a new way of being in the world.

Every morning, first thing, I sat cross-legged on a thick round cushion called a zafu, started the relaxation course audio tape, and stared at the wall in our living room for forty-five minutes. Daniel's slow, precise voice guided the meditation and periodically reminded me to focus on my breath.

"If you get distracted, do not blame yourself. Do not judge. Simply return your attention to your breathing. Feel the breath filling and then emptying from your abdomen."

It's disturbing how virulent, how insidious the mind can be. Depending on the day, I might not even make it a minute before my mind kicked in and distracted me with its seductive frenzy of trivial thoughts. What did I have on my agenda for the day? Would Dr. Pali ever return my calls? What renal-friendly food should I make for breakfast? For lunch? Did the dog need a walk? Was this a waste of time?

Then, Daniel's voice would penetrate through the noise in my head and I'd remember to focus on my breathing, for the next minute or so. No wonder Daniel called it "a practice." It required so much effort to not think, to not let my mind run its endless harangue. My first meditation experiences left me exhausted.

The One Constant

The third session of the relaxation course came at the end of January and found me at the breaking point. I was still working full time, my blood pressure was surging, and my neck pain was making sleep an ordeal. This was also the time when each new blood pressure drug I tried made me feel like a human guinea pig, enduring the negative side effects of each.

"At least I managed to make it to class on time," I thought as I rushed into the room.

Daniel had everyone sit on chairs in a circle. He had each of us introduce ourselves and explain to the group why we were there.

When my turn came, I had a strange, out-of-body experience. I had never spoken about my circumstances to a group of strangers, and I found myself trying to control my emotions and remain objective, distancing myself from what I was saying. It felt as if I were describing someone else.

"Hi, I'm Lisa. I have end stage renal disease."

The puzzled looks on some faces told me that they didn't understand this clinical phrase, so I backed up to explain in more detail, but then my control began to slip.

"My kidneys don't work anymore. A rare autoimmune disease destroyed them. I'm on dialysis now."

Speaking the words made everything feel too real.

"I hope this class will help me deal." I broke off lamely, overcome by tears.

The woman beside me handed over the box of tissues that was making the rounds. My tears subsided as I listened to the woman introduce herself and describe the chronic migraines she suffered and how she hoped to alleviate them through stress reduction. The circle was almost complete when a well-dressed man wearing a pager began to speak.

"Please call me Carl," the man told us.

DIALYSIS: A MEMOIR

I recognized him, but his name wasn't "Carl." He was one of the doctors in Dr. Pali's nephrology group. He looked around the circle while he spoke but avoided looking at me.

"I'm being treated for cancer and I'm experiencing some stress."

He didn't elaborate as did some of the others, who rambled on at length about their physical and mental suffering. I found it hard to believe he had cancer. He looked healthy, and despite a receding hairline, it didn't look like he'd undergone chemotherapy. He reminded me of my own situation and how you can't always judge a person's health by their outward appearance.

Before Daniel had us lie on the floor for another meditation session, "Carl" approached me.

"Hi Lisa," he said. "You probably wonder why I'm not using my real name."

He fumbled with his hands in his pockets and didn't quite meet my gaze. Was he embarrassed? Ashamed?

"None of the other docs or patients knows about my cancer. I hope you won't mention you saw me here to anyone." His blue eyes finally met mine.

It was obvious that if he'd known someone in the course would recognize him he never would have enrolled. I thought of Dr. Pali and the other doctors in the nephrology group, always so well groomed and in control, so apparently infallible. He needed this course as much as I did.

"Don't worry," I promised. "I won't say anything."

Daniel had us find places to lie on the floor. He turned off the lights and told us to focus on our breathing.

Between the stabbing neck pain and the violent headache that had plagued me since I'd started the latest round of blood pressure drugs, I found it difficult to focus. The uncomfortable pounding of my heart, another side effect of the drugs, was exacerbated by lying stretched full length on the floor.

As I lay there suffering, a surge of rage suddenly overcame me, an emotion I hadn't once experienced since being hospitalized. It startled me and overpowered me with its strength. I wanted to scream: Why the fuck is all this happening to me? Why can't the doctors make me better?

Instead, I yelled, "I can't take this anymore!" and staggered to my feet.

My heart lurched painfully, a cold sweat broke over my body, and I lunged for the hallway door. I needed to get the hell away. I wanted to run, to flee, to escape the horror that had become my life.

The most I managed was a fast walk toward the elevator. Daniel reached me before it arrived.

"You can do it," he said. "Stay with your breath."

His slow, precise voice annoyed me and I wanted to tell him to shut up, but I didn't, because I was also touched that he'd cared enough to come after me.

I took a deep breath. I exhaled. I did it again. I wiped the tears from my face and breathed in again. I exhaled. The rage was gone and my anger dissipated. I followed him back into the conference room.

I lay down again among the other people, embarrassed by my outburst. There was nowhere to run, I realized. I couldn't escape what was now my life. But I could breathe.

That night, I began to see that even in the throes of overwhelming emotion I still breathed. By being mindful of my breath, I could step briefly outside emotional and physical sensations to focus on another plane of reality, one that calmly, reassuringly, repeated itself over and over again.

Everything else in my life might be up for grabs, but my breath would always be with me, as long as I lived. It was the one constant, the one grounding force. Daniel was right. I could do it.

The next day, Daniel came to visit me at the dialysis clinic. He was a member of the hospital staff, so he was allowed onto the dialysis floor.

"I wanted to make sure you are OK," he said.

I apologized, still embarrassed by my behavior, but he was sympathetic.

"Your feelings are understandable, considering how much you're going through right now."

To pass the time, he told me his story. He'd once been a successful businessman living on the East Coast, a graduate of Cornell. Then, several years ago, he took a two-month vacation with a friend to a remote region of Alaska. One day, as they were making their way slowly up a steep, trail-less canyon with tundra-covered peaks looming above, he had a revelation. In that moment, he realized his whole life had gone off-course and that he hadn't been living with integrity or consistent with his conscience.

When he returned from Alaska, he settled his accounts on the East Coast, moved to California, and began studying how to help other people. He trained with other Buddhists and practitioners of mindfulness meditation, including Jon Kabbat Zinn, the founder and director of the Stress Reduction Clinic at the University of Massachusetts Medical Center for Mind/Body Medicine. It was from Zinn that Daniel developed his own relaxation course, which aimed to offer alternatives to traditional methods for dealing with stress and chronic pain.

It impressed me that Daniel had taken time out of his schedule to come and visit me at the clinic. Unlike the harried doctors and nurses, and certainly unlike my rapid-fire PR colleagues, Daniel moved in harmony with his own will. He didn't behave as though the external world drove him to act. While his slow way of talking and moving continued to irritate me, I now saw that they were integral to his philosophy. He moved through life mindfully.

His belief in my own ability to develop mindfulness inspired me, and his course profoundly and permanently changed my attitude and approach to life.

Before the relaxation course, taking time to experience specific sensations in my body was unthinkable. Taking time to not do anything at all was beyond unthinkable. I'd honed my life to an intensely narrow focus on speed and efficiency. My whole approach centered on these two qualities.

Everything I did was fast and efficient, from my high tech PR job to my hard-core biking and workouts, even to such mundane things as grocery shopping and cleaning house. The goal was to get as much done as possible in the shortest amount of time.

The first month on dialysis made me violate these principles because dialysis forced me to sit still in one place and because it left me too exhausted to do anything while I was hooked up. In essence, dialysis forced me to waste time, which stressed me out. To cope with the stress, I started using the tools I learned in the relaxation course. As my meditation practice deepened and as I adjusted to dialysis, my perspective started to change—speed and efficiency no longer dominated my life.

Removed by my condition from the world of the healthy, I experienced a strange combination of conflicting emotions. On the one hand, I felt jealous of healthy, "normal" people. As I sat mindlessly watching the cable TV over my dialysis chair, I felt rage at all the energetic healthy people on the shows, people who lived free of the regulations imposed on me. I looked at my family and friends, at all the other people out there, and felt the horrible injustice of my condition.

And yet, at the same time, I experienced a surprising sense of freedom. It was as if my no longer being "normal" released me from the obligations I had imposed on myself. Speed and efficiency, concerns about money and being successful, the pressures of my job, all those things that healthy people worry about, as I had, no longer mattered so much. I felt free to live my life, day by day. Beyond the hassles of hemodialysis and my physical problems, I grew mindful and appreciative of the simpler aspects of life, from the regular flow of my breath and a good night's rest to the gentle warmth of the winter sun on my face. As it turned out, I learned mindfulness meditation just in time to cope with the next crisis.

Chapter 6 - Murphy's Law

Peritoneal Dialysis

My experience with hemodialysis did not improve over time. My blood pressure remained achingly high, my body debilitated and wrung out after each dialysis session, and I continued to feel frustrated by the clinic's inefficiencies and my own powerlessness to change the system and improve my course of treatment. In early February, Dr. Pali suggested I switch from hemodialysis to peritoneal dialysis, another form of treatment, which she felt would be less traumatic to my body.

Compared to hemodialysis, peritoneal dialysis seemed a much better alternative. I would be able to do it myself, on my own time, and in the privacy of my own home. No longer would my care rest in the hands of others, and no longer would I be at the mercy of other people's schedules and priorities. I wouldn't have to take time out from work, and on peritoneal dialysis, I'd be in charge of both the conditions and the safety of my care. I eagerly looked forward to regaining some control over my life.

Unlike hemodialysis, which relies on machines, peritoneal dialysis relies on the peritoneal membrane, an extra membrane encasing the organs of the body to achieve dialysis.

The peritoneal membrane originally evolved as an extra line of defense to protect the body against contamination from diseased or ruptured organs. Its existence was first recorded by observers of the mutilated bodies of ancient Roman gladiators. Peritoneal dialysis was first performed on a human in 1923, but it didn't become a standard treatment option for kidney patients until the mid 1960s, when doctors developed a catheter that could be surgically implanted into a person's abdomen and used repeatedly with minimal risk of infection.

Peritoneal dialysis involves filling the peritoneal cavity with a solution called dialysate, much like sugar water, and letting it sit in the body for an extended period of time. Because the dialysate has a different chemistry from the organs, it harnesses the natural process of osmosis to "pull" toxins and fluids through the peritoneal membrane and into the peritoneal cavity. After a period of time and before equilibrium is established between the two mediums, the dialysate is removed and new dialysate is put in, beginning the process all over again.

In order for me to start peritoneal dialysis, I'd need a peritoneal catheter.

One day in February, as I sat hooked up at the clinic, Dr. Pali and a visiting specialist stopped by to discuss the upcoming catheter surgery.

"We've pioneered a new laparoscopic technique for inserting the catheter," the specialist explained. "Instead of performing full abdominal surgery, we use scopes for viewing inside the body and we perform the surgery using probes."

"There are important advantages," Dr. Pali jumped in, excited. "You'll have a lot less pain if you have a laparoscopy, and you'll only have a small horizontal scar on your left side, only an inch long," she held up her fingers to illustrate how small the scar would be, "rather than a long vertical scar down the center of your abdomen."

"That does sound better," I agreed.

"And with laparoscopy, you'll only have to stay in the hospital for one night. Your recovery will be much faster, too," she added.

The one drawback they quickly glossed over was the fact that I'd be Dr. Pali's first patient to undergo the procedure. Though he would observe Dr. Pali during the surgery, the laparoscopic specialist wouldn't perform the operation himself. I didn't want to serve as Dr. Pali's guinea pig, but I also didn't want to undergo full abdominal surgery. I agreed to the procedure.

Murphy's Law

DIALYSIS: A MEMOIR

Murphy's Law states that if anything can go wrong, it will. With all the troubles I'd had on hemodialysis and with the blood pressure drugs, I should have realized that Murphy's Law was running my life. Looking back now, I can't help but think I was cursed with some kind of extraordinarily bad luck.

The laparoscopic surgery, conducted on a Monday morning in mid-February, was relatively painless and seemed a success. It left me sporting a twelve-inch rubber tube that protruded from the left side of my abdomen and ended in a two-inch long nozzle, which consisted of a valve and disposable cap for hooking me up to the peritoneal dialysis (PD) machine.

But then the trouble started. While recovering from the procedure, I developed a numb sensation on my tongue. When I mentioned it to the attending nephrologist, she was concerned.

"I have no idea what could be causing such a sensation," she said. "It doesn't correlate with any of the adverse reactions reported for the medications you're currently taking." She paused, a frown creasing her brow. "I think you'd better see a neurologist to make sure something else isn't going on."

Unfortunately, the neurologist wasn't available until late Tuesday, which meant I was stuck in the hospital another day. I had my Tuesday dialysis at the inpatient unit while I waited. The neurologist finally came late, after Kurt had gone home for the night. She spoke with a distinct New York accent, her manner authoritative.

"A numb tongue is not a symptom of a drug allergy, but it may be indicative of a serious neurological problem. I'll schedule you for an MRI immediately and be in touch as soon as I have the results."

I lay back on the hospital bed after she left, thinking, What next? I already had a virulent autoimmune disease that had killed my kidneys and turned my world upside down. Was there some new disease lurking, about to be discovered?

After the MRI on Wednesday morning, I spent the rest of the day anxiously waiting for the results to come back. By that night, however, I still hadn't heard anything from the neurologist. On Thursday morning, as I finished the basic hospital breakfast of cold bagel, cream cheese, hard boiled eggs, and tea, the neurologist called, sounding cheerful.

"Your MRI results were negative," she said. "You're perfectly fine. You can go home today."

Relieved, I patiently waited for the discharge papers to arrive. Several hours passed during which I had another inpatient dialysis session. By early afternoon, I was growing impatient when the doctor suddenly walked into the room, her face tight.

"Something has come up. Your MRI indicates an anomaly. It looks like there might be a blood clot in one of the veins at the base of your brain."

Stunned, I stared at her. How could something that started out as a simple catheter operation mushroom into a possible life-threatening brain condition?

"I'm going to order an ultrasound, which will help us see more clearly if this is indeed the case," she said.

The moment she left, I called Kurt to tell him the shocking news.

"But didn't the neurologist just say you were fine and could go home? Why would she suddenly contradict herself?" He was suspicious.

"I don't know. The whole thing's bizarre. My tongue's not even numb anymore, but what if something really is wrong with my brain?" To myself I thought, with my luck something probably is.

"OK, that's it," Kurt said, hearing my fear. "I'll leave work and come wait with you for the results."

He arrived in time to accompany me to the ultrasound, a quick and painless procedure, and then we returned to the hospital room to wait. The neurologist called within the hour.

"The ultrasound is normal," she said. "You're fine."

Too overcome with relief to think of asking any questions, I hung up and told Kurt the good news. He was appalled.

DIALYSIS: A MEMOIR

"Unbelievable! How could those two tests be so contradictory? It doesn't make sense," he frowned, thinking. "I'll bet she confused your MRI results with someone else's. You've got to get better doctors! I'm going to find you some!"

"Sure," I shrugged. I couldn't think about the future. I was just thankful my brain was apparently OK and I could go home.

After two extra days in the hospital, I finally went home on Thursday night, hoping everything was OK. I was wrong.

Friday evening, as we prepared dinner for some friends, I felt something warm against my abdomen. To my horror, the end of the catheter was wet. The damned thing was leaking! Terrified I'd get an infection, since a leak meant there was an open access point into my body, we had to drop our dinner preparations, send our guests home, and rush off to the ER.

I dreaded going to the ER on a weekend night. I'd learned from experience that Friday and Saturday nights were the worst, swamped with everything from injured drunks and victims of assault to mothers delivering babies. That particular night was also a full moon, and we'd learned from my favorite ER doctor that full moons seem to increase the number of ER patients. Unfortunately, he wasn't working that night, so I was eventually seen by another doctor just before midnight. Following his instructions, the worn-looking ER nurse cursorily taped a tight, temporary seal over the catheter's leaky valve, since the ER didn't have any PD valves.

"I'll give you some prophylactic antibiotics," she said. "But you should make sure and see the peritoneal dialysis (PD) nurse at the clinic tomorrow to have your catheter fixed."

Kurt waited with me for another hour while I received the antibiotic IV drip.

First thing Saturday morning, I went to the El Cerrito branch of the for-profit dialysis chain, since my own clinic was closed on weekends. The PD nurse was intelligent, friendly, and efficient, quickly snipping off the faulty valve and replacing it with a new one. She exclaimed over my bad luck, saying that it was quite rare for catheters to leak.

As I prepared to leave, I looked about the PD clinic, a small room adjacent to the hemodialysis clinic. Everything seemed to run smoothly and efficiently.

"Do you think I could switch to this clinic?" I asked hopefully.

"I'm sorry," the nurse said. "We have no room. Both our hemodialysis and our peritoneal dialysis units are completely filled."

I left, cursing my bad luck. The leaky catheter, the mediocre Berkeley clinic—it all made me feel shaky and unsure about the new world of PD I was about to enter. When would Murphy's Law stop running my life?

PD Training

My body needed time to heal after the laparoscopy, so I couldn't begin peritoneal dialysis right away. I continued a week longer on hemodialysis While I waited, I began PD training.

Perusing the training manual, I realized I could learn the material in an hour, so I was irritated to learn that I'd have to take a week off from work for the training. I tried to persuade the PD nurse to shorten the training schedule, but she refused, obstinately citing protocol.

Unlike the bustling hemodialysis clinic downstairs, the PD clinic felt vacant. The PD nurse didn't seem busy, and I rarely saw any other PD patients. The place was so quiet. There was no blaring Musak, no TV, no beeping hemodialysis machinery, no banter among the nurses and patients, and except for the faint smell of the new carpeting and the slight scent of sterile alcohol, the place was odorless. The PD clinic was so calm and orderly that I was surprised to find myself thinking it felt lonely. Hemodialysis had been such a communal, public experience. Peritoneal dialysis was going to be different.

PD training began with learning sterile technique, since the biggest problem for patients is developing either peritonitis or infections of the exit site, the place where the catheter leaves the body. The training started with gathering the supplies, microwaving the bag of dialysate to warm it to body temperature, and closing the door of the exam room. I then thoroughly washed my hands, donned a surgical mask, and took hold of the attachment line to the dialysate bag with its plug in my right hand and a mock catheter valve in my left. The trick was being able to keep hold of both tubes while I quickly and smoothly popped the sterile plug off the attachment line to the dialysate bag with my left hand, disposed of the catheter cap with my right hand, and then used both hands to screw the mock catheter end into the attachment line. Nothing non-sterile was to touch either the catheter end or the open end of the line leading to the dialysate bag.

The next part of PD training involved performing continuous ambulatory peritoneal dialysis on myself. To do this, I used my own catheter line for the first time, hooking myself up to a bag of dialysate, then suspending the bag on an IV pole above my head to let gravity pull the dialysate solution into my peritoneal cavity. The PD nurse watched me perform the sterile technique. Everything seemed to be working. The dialysate, which I'd previously warmed in the microwave for a minute, created a strangely warm sensation as it filled my peritoneal cavity. The bag contained 1.5 liters, so by the time it had all entered my abdomen, I felt bloated and uncomfortable, as though I'd eaten a huge meal.

The nurse wanted me to sit for several hours to let the solution perform its dialyzing function. Fortunately, I'd brought a press release to work on. Once the time was up, I clamped off the line leading to the fill bag and unclamped the line leading to the drain bag that lay on the floor by my feet. The idea was that once I opened the clamp to the drain line gravity would pull the fluid out of my body and down into the bag on the floor.

At first everything seemed to work OK, but then, just a quarter of the way through the process, the draining stopped. Panicked, I called the nurse into the room. She had me move around to see if I could dislodge whatever might be blocking or clogging the catheter. I tried bending over. I tried jumping vigorously up and down. She tried flowing more dialysate into me to see if that might clear the catheter. Nothing worked, so she called Dr. Pali. In the meantime, I went back to work and spent an uncomfortable afternoon with a huge volume of dialysate distending my gut.

Another Hospital Stay

The end result of the blocked catheter was that Dr. Pali sent me back to the hospital for full abdominal surgery so the doctors could get inside my abdomen and see why the catheter wasn't working. As I'd feared, abdominal surgery wasn't fun. In preparation, I had to have two enemas, an experience not worth recounting. The general anesthesia plus the pain medication after the surgery made me unable to sleep, because every time I started to doze off, it felt like my body was forgetting to breathe. I'd jerk myself awake and remind myself to inhale. Each time this happened, I'd lie there terrified that I'd almost died. The drugs finally wore off about 3 a.m. and I managed to fall asleep, despite the red, throbbing haze of abdominal pain.

During the procedure, the surgeon discovered I had an "omentum wrap." It turns out that in addition to the peritoneum, our bodies have developed another line of defense called the omentum, a free-floating membrane that can wrap itself around objects the body identifies as alien, thereby protecting the body by sealing off the alien object. My omentum had done just that, wrapping itself around the catheter to protect my body from it. The surgeon had to perform an "omentumectomy" and cut off the piece of omentum wrapped around the catheter.

Later, when Dr. Pali and the laparoscopic specialist came to check up on me, I quizzed them about the laparoscopy.

"The limited visibility of our scopes keeps us from being able to see a patient's omentum during a laparoscopy," the specialist explained. "We make sure to implant the catheter in a place where the omentum can't reach it. In all the surgeries I've conducted, I've never had this problem. Unfortunately, in your case, you had an extraordinarily long omentum."

Just my luck, I thought as I listened to him. Murphy's Law was still running my life. After the doctors left, I lay pressing the pillow hard to my stomach to assuage the pain and feeling both angry and helpless at the same time. On the one hand, the doctor's explanation frustrated me—I'd gained nothing by being Dr. Pali's guinea pig. But I also felt defeated, as though the world had it in for me and that there was nothing I could do but endure each new problem thrown my way. The good news was that after all the trials and tribulations of having the catheter inserted, it now seemed to finally work. By April, I finally switched to peritoneal dialysis, and Murphy's Law lost its grip on my life.

Chapter 7 - PD Life

PD Paraphernalia

I had high hopes for peritoneal dialysis (PD). After everything I'd gone through on hemodialysis, PD had to be better. Dr. Pali, along with most of the literature I'd read, suggested that people on PD could lead much more "normal" lives than people on hemodialysis, because they didn't have to travel to a clinic three times a week for treatment. PD would put me in control of everything: from storing and maintaining the supplies and equipment to performing the actual dialysis. It felt good to finally be able to do something about my own care.

The company that manufactured the dialysate delivered a month's allotment of supplies at a time. I'd been warned there would be a lot of boxes, but I was still surprised by the large number brought one morning in April by a burly man dressed in the company's navy blue uniform.

"I'm glad you could get here before I have to leave for work," I said.

"Where do you want 'em?" The man stacked five boxes on the dolly.

"In the garage. Follow me." I led the way down the driveway. "Can you stack them for me? I'd stack them myself, but I can't strain my gut with all this dialysate in it."

"Sure thing." The man set to work stacking thirty boxes, each about one and a half feet wide by two and a half feet long, into the space Kurt and I had cleared over the weekend.

Each box had color-coded adhesive tape attached to it, in addition to the printed information, to help clearly identify which dialysate concentration the box held. Yellow signaled boxes of 1.5% concentrate, green 2.5%, and red 4.25%. Most of the boxes contained two big six-liter bags for use overnight with the cycler, and most were green because I'd use that concentrate the most. The other boxes held six each of the two-liter bags I'd need for my afternoon exchanges.

I looked at my watch. It was pushing nine o'clock. At this rate, I was going to be late to work.

"Wow, that's a lot of boxes!" I exclaimed, hoping to convey my thanks for the man's hard work and speed him up. Fortunately, our garage was large enough that the boxes only filled one corner of the space.

"There are still a few more." The man steadily wheeled in a final batch, small beads of sweat shining on his dark brow.

Some of the boxes contained the "cassettes." I'd need a new cassette each night in order to connect the dialysate bags to the cycler and the cycler to myself. A cassette consisted of a plastic brace and held a bunch of tubing. Another smaller set of boxes contained the disposable caps I'd need to seal my catheter off each time I unhooked from the machine. The last box was crammed full of disposable paper surgical masks, sterile pads for covering my exit site (where the catheter left my body), tape for securing the catheter against my body, and a huge number of individually sealed alcohol wipes and a bottle of hydrogen peroxide for cleaning my exit site.

I tried to hurry the man down the driveway, but he paused outside his truck and looked thoughtfully at me.

"My cousin's kidneys are failing and he's gonna have to go on dialysis. How is it for you?"

Of all the things I could imagine him asking me, this wasn't one of them. I was stressed about being late to work, but I couldn't just rush off without talking to him.

"There's been a steep learning curve, and to be honest, it hasn't been all that easy. I didn't like hemodialysis, so I'm switching to peritoneal dialysis. Hopefully, it'll go better. At least I'm alive. If dialysis didn't exist, I'd be dead, so I'm thankful for that."

I unlocked my car. "Thanks for your help with all those boxes. I hope your cousin is OK."

The man nodded and rolled the dolly up the truck's loading ramp.

On my drive to work, I thought about the delivery man and his cousin. I'd been so wrapped up in my own private drama that I'd been blind yet again to the other worlds outside my own. I remembered Leon and Maisie, Natalie and Delia and the other people at the hemodialysis clinic. There was a whole world out there of people dealing with the effects of kidney failure.

Later, as I sat in my office and reviewed my day's itinerary, the juxtaposition of my work worries with these life-and-death thoughts made me feel schizophrenic. There was no way to reconcile the two worlds.

I never did find out what happened to the man's cousin. The next month's dialysate shipment was delivered by someone else, who told me he'd been transferred.

The following day, the cycler arrived. It weighed upwards of forty pounds and, though it came with a carrying case, I wasn't sure how I'd manage to travel with it.

Simple in design, it consisted of a flat warmer bed, on which a six-liter bag of dialysate would sit and be warmed to my body temperature. On its side was a digital display, four buttons for programming it, and a compartment for loading the cassette into place. To work properly, it had to be located close to where I slept and at approximately the same height as my body. I also needed extra space for a second six-liter bag, since I would use two bags (twelve liters of dialysate) each night.

When Kurt came home from work that night, I asked him for help rearranging our small bedroom.

"Can you help slide the bed over?" I needed more space on my side for the equipment.

"But then the bed is out of alignment with the windows."

Moving the bed would also throw off the artistic arrangement of his favorite digital photos that he'd precisely positioned across the room from the bed.

"I know, but we've gotta get the machine set up here. Can you help arrange these?" I pointed to four boxes of red

4.25% dialysate, the strongest concentration and the one I'd use least.

"How's this?" Kurt stacked them to create a platform on which to stand the cycler.

"Looking good." I lugged the cycler into place and cleared space on top of the bedside table for the second bag of dialysate. I stored a set of the other necessary supplies in a drawer by the bed.

"How's that?" I stood back and looked with satisfaction at the arrangement.

Kurt studied his artwork and the alignment of the bed. "It's OK," he shrugged, and then went into the living room to watch Star Trek.

His lack of enthusiasm didn't sway me. Beauty might be his organizing principle, but functionality has always been mine. I felt better. Everything I needed for PD was in its place, and I felt an invigorating sense of control.

The Nightly Routine

The first step of what was to become my ten-hour nightly routine for the next year involved priming the cycler. I reviewed the notes I'd taken during PD training and at 7:45 p.m. began the preparations.

First, I removed two of the six-liter bags from a box. Then, after thoroughly washing my hands, I ripped open the plastic outer wrapping that protected each bag. I laid the bag on the bed, wiped off the condensation, pushed hard on the bag to check for leaks, and inspected the solution to ensure its clarity, since cloudiness indicates contamination.

Once sure the bags were in good condition, I placed one on the cycler and the other beside it on the bedside table. I then closed the bedroom door to prevent possible contamination from air flow and donned one of the surgical masks. I pressed the "Go" button on the cycler and the digital command read: "Load the Cassette." I discarded the cassette's protective outer plastic shell, opened the panel on the front of the cycler, and loaded the cassette, making sure each of its five tubes lined up correctly in its blue plastic brace.

Now came one of the trickier parts of the procedure: "spiking" the bags of dialysate. I leafed through the PD instruction manual and reviewed the detailed steps one more time before I set about spiking my first bag. My breath grew uncomfortably warm, trapped against my face by the surgical mask. To relieve my anxiety, I reminded myself that if I screwed up, I could always throw the components away and start over.

To spike the bag, I first sealed off the main part of each dialysate bag by using a blue plastic clamp on the bag's narrow, plugged end. I then took the tube from the cassette that corresponded to the dialysate bag on the cycler and popped off the bag's plug. Spiking involved shoving the pointed sterile end of the cassette tube into the sterile narrow opening of the dialysate bag. It was a tight fit and shoving them together meant the risk of slipping. If the sterile ends touched anything but each other, I'd potentially become infected. This time, I succeeded in spiking the bag and maintaining sterile conditions. I repeated the spiking procedure for the second bag, heaved a sigh of relief when I succeeded in doing that, and then removed the blue plastic clamps from each of the dialysate bags.

The final step to prepare the cycler was to connect the cassette to the drain line, since once the cycler began draining me, the used dialysate would need someplace to go. Because my sleeping spot was so far from the bathroom, I used one of the special fifteen-foot drain line extenders to reach the toilet. (This worked fine until we acquired a kitten several months later. MaxCat found the extender tube winding into the bathroom irresistibly fascinating and, after his clawing through the tube and spilling sticky dialysate all over the bathroom floor, I resorted to using a painter's bucket big enough to handle the twelve or so liters of used dialysate at the end of each night's dialysis.)

DIALYSIS: A MEMOIR

This preparation took fifteen minutes. Then I pressed the green "Go" button once more. The digital readout now said "Priming," and the cycler began to warm the bag of dialysate on it and check the functioning of all the lines by pumping a small amount of dialysate through the cassette and out the drain line. If there'd been a problem (like those times I forgot to remove the blue plastic clamps from the bags of dialysate after spiking them), the machine would let out piercing beeps, but this first time, everything ran smoothly.

I got ready for bed while the cycler primed. I weighed myself to the half-pound on the accurate medical scale the dialysate company had sent me, took my blood pressure, and recorded the values on the flow sheet, which I was to bring to my monthly PD clinic visits.

Because I no longer urinated, the fluid I consumed was pulled into my peritoneal cavity by the dialysate, where it pooled and caused my abdomen, "my gut" as I called it, to bulge. Tonight, my weight was up six pounds. Though this might seem like a lot of extra fluid for someone with two functioning kidneys, it was still a smaller amount than the fluid fluctuations I'd experienced when I was on hemodialysis and only dialyzed every other day. I was also glad to see that my blood pressure had come down.

After recording the information, I washed my hands a second time, once again donned the surgical mask, and then performed the riskiest act of all: hooking up. I knew at this point that if I screwed up and contaminated my catheter, I'd have to go to ER, wait endless hours, and get a prophylactic batch of antibiotics, which could lead potentially to antibiotic resistance.

I managed not to think about all these risks by forcing myself to focus minutely on each action. I popped off the end of the cassette's tube and unscrewed the disposable cap of my catheter. I held my breath at the instant my naked catheter end was exposed to the open air and then, as quickly as possible, connected the tube.

LISA FRIEDEN

With so many steps involved and with such manual dexterity required, I could see why PD isn't viable for arthritic patients or people lacking manual dexterity or even good eyesight. (Thankfully, in the year I was on PD, I never developed peritonitis, though I did once develop an exit site infection that required antibiotics.)

Finally, I pressed the green "Start" button and the digital command read "Drain 1 of 6." The first of six drain cycles began. Once hooked up to the machine, I lay in bed and read, though the tubing was long enough for me to walk about my side of the bedroom if I wanted.

As my abdominal area shrank, I experienced a strange, light feeling of emptiness. Toward the end of the drain cycle, the sensation gave way to strong abdominal spasms as the cycler strained to suck out every drop of the used dialysate. I sat hunched on the side of the bed in an effort to allay the discomfort, similar to intestinal or menstrual cramps. The first cycle drained me completely dry, whereas the later five cycles would only remove about 75% of the used dialysate.

Just when I thought I couldn't stand it anymore, the cycler abruptly switched to "Fill 1 of 6." I felt relief as my abdomen began to swell with the warmed dialysate solution. Bigger and bigger my gut swelled, past the two-liter comfort level, until two and a half liters were crammed in, leaving me feeling uncomfortably bloated.

At this point, I developed a roiling sensation in my stomach and a burning at the back of my throat. The pressure of the dialysate on my stomach and esophagus caused nasty heartburn. A spastic burst of coughing ripped through me and it felt like I was going to throw up my dinner. Fortunately, I didn't vomit, but the coughing jag left me tired and shaky. (After a few weeks of this coughing, I discovered that cough drops soothed the spasms, and I lived on them for most of the year I was on PD.)

Once done filling, the cycler pump switched off and the digital command read "Dwell 1 of 6." For the next hour, the dialysate "dwelled" inside me, allowing time for the dialysate to pull toxins and fluid from my organs through the peritoneal membrane and into my peritoneal cavity, until the next drain cycle began.

My first night sleeping on the cycler was rough. The round of blood pressure drugs I took before bed knocked me out for the first four hours, but then at 2 a.m., the cycler jolted Kurt and me awake with its obnoxious beeping.

"What the hell!" I muttered, barely conscious as I rolled over and looked at the machine. The readout glowed: "Check Line."

"Close your eyes," I whispered to Kurt. "I've gotta turn on the light."

I switched on the bedside lamp and grabbed the cycler's user manual. There were no obvious reasons why the machine was unhappy. After reviewing the trouble-shooting tips, I realized I must have rolled over on my catheter and crimped the line, which must have prevented the cycler from starting its next drain cycle.

I pressed the green "Go" button, and sure enough, the cycler uttered its faint gurgling sound as it once again began sucking the dialysate from me. The quiet repetitious sound, like an aquarium, helped me fall back asleep, though I woke again at 4 a.m. when the cycler sucked too hard on my gut.

At 6:30 a.m. I awoke, tired and bleary-eyed, when the cycler's blaring alarm signaled my dialysis time was complete. Kurt didn't look refreshed, either. I told him to hold his breath while I disconnected from the cycler. Stuffed with two liters of fresh dialysate, I was alive and ready to start the day, if barely.

The nightly dialysis routine distanced me from Kurt. I typically made it home from work by 6:30 p.m., but he rarely got home before 8 p.m. His commute took almost an hour, and since he worked for a start-up, he was expected to put in long hours. Before PD, I'd waited for him for dinner, but once on PD, I had to eat as soon as possible, since I needed time to prime the machine and because I couldn't eat too close to hook up time or risk vomiting or suffering violent coughing jags. By the time Kurt got home, I was already preparing for bed, and by the time he'd eaten dinner, I was already isolated in our bedroom, hooked up to the machine with the door closed to maintain sterile conditions.

As the first month on PD progressed, Kurt and I adapted to our new circumstances. When my nightly coughing didn't abate, Kurt started sleeping one work night a week in the guest bedroom across the hall. I didn't mind. In fact, I felt relieved on those nights because I didn't have to worry about waking him with my coughing.

I also came to feel that evenings after work weren't so bad. After a chaotic day of PR politics and logistics, I found I enjoyed some time alone. Rather than feel dissatisfied with the situation, Kurt and I resumed the hobbies we'd left on the back burner when we were healthy and too busy for them. Kurt retired to the office in the garage and deepened his expertise in digital photography. I hadn't read any serious literature since finishing my English PhD, but now I began to read again. We made the best of our circumstances. Even with all the hassles, it was, finally, OK. It had to be.

2:30 p.m. - Afternoon Dialysis

My daily dialysis regimen also included a mid-afternoon exchange that took about thirty minutes. I didn't use the cycler for this and I could do it almost anywhere. I'd warm up one of the small two-liter bags of dialysate in a microwave or, when camping, in a dialysate warmer that plugged into the car's cigarette lighter. I either hung the bag from my IV pole, which I wheeled into work each week and left in my office, or from the car window. I untangled the drain line and laid the empty drain bag on the floor. Once connected, I opened my catheter and gravity pulled the used dialysate down into the drain bag. This draining process took about twenty minutes. I could read, meditate, or continue working if I was at work. After draining, I clamped the drain line off, cracked the seal of the fresh two-liter bag hanging above, and let the new dialysate flow into me.

No one at work commented or made any sign of noticing what I was doing, but my afternoon exchanges set me apart. Everyone left their doors open unless they were in a meeting or on a conference call. My door had almost always remained open and I used to enjoy the easy camaraderie we all shared. Now, I had to set the alarm clock on my watch each day to remind myself to stop whatever I was doing and prepare for PD. Closing my office door at 2:30 p.m. signaled to everyone that I was hooked up and my office was off limits.

Where hemodialysis had removed me from the office and left me feeling distanced from my co-workers, the afternoon PD sessions made the separation tangibly real. Cara and I could still chat and conduct business over the speakerphone, but the shut door loomed large. When 2:30 p.m. came, I had to stop working—not an easy thing to do when the stock market soared and high tech PR stood center stage.

Food Fury

Unlike people on hemodialysis who only dialyze every other day, people on PD dialyze constantly, and because of this, they can eat a more varied diet. Potassium-rich foods like potatoes, tomatoes, and citrus can cause cardiac arrest in hemodialysis patients, but PD patients can eat potassium in moderation. Steak and donuts had long since lost their appeal. Hemodialysis had left me too tired to cook or even to lust for food, so when I first switched to PD, I looked forward to adding tomatoes, potatoes and other potassium-rich foods to my diet.

Once on PD, however, I found I still couldn't eat my favorite foods, all of which were too high in phosphorus. Dairy products, chocolate, nuts, and beans were all off limits. If I ate them, I risked developing osteoporosis. Because most food contains some amount of phosphorus, I had to chew chalky calcium tablets whenever I ate anything in order to introduce an alternative source of calcium into my system (besides my bones) for neutralizing the phosphorus.

Unfortunately, too much calcium built up in my blood over time, an unhealthy condition called hypercalcemia, so the doctors started me on a newly developed medication, Renagel. Though Renagel didn't elevate my calcium levels, it also didn't bind phosphorus as well as the calcium supplements, and it led to no end of embarrassment and discomfort, causing burbly unsettled bowels and rank flatulence.

Before kidney failure, my diet rarely focused on meat, which I'd used primarily as a condiment to lend flavor to the other ingredients in meals. PD patients lose a lot of protein during dialysis and I was strongly encouraged to eat meat. Eggs every breakfast, endless chicken sandwiches for lunch, and meat-packed dinners disgusted me. Kurt, who grew up in Indiana, enjoyed what amounted to a traditional American diet, but I resented the restrictions dialysis imposed on my eating habits.

Most of the time I wanted to optimize my health and be the perfect PD patient, but sometimes I felt ready to snap under the weight of all the restraints and controls imposed on my behavior. I have always been a chocoholic, but once on dialysis and out of concern for my bones, I denied myself the pleasure.

Imagine my chagrin, my utter dismay, when I found myself confronted one evening by trays of Joseph Schmidt gourmet truffles! Kurt and I had gone to a housewarming party in San Francisco hosted by a friend of ours. It just so happened that his landlord was a friend of Joseph Schmidt, one of San Francisco's elite chocolatiers.

Having not eaten a single bite of chocolate in over four months, I told myself, "I will eat just one." Dark chocolate, Grand Marnier, Kahlua, Irish Crème, the tray of truffles sitting among the other party treats beckoned. My hand reached forward.

Kurt frowned. "You're not supposed to eat that."

DIALYSIS: A MEMOIR

"I know, I know. I'll just have one, OK? I think this is dark chocolate." I picked up the dark brown truffle.

Before Kurt could make another disapproving comment, I bit into the large, decadent truffle. My God! It may sound like a cliché to say that chocolate stimulates something almost sexual in women, but when that first bite slid over my tongue and down my throat, it not only tasted unbelievably delicious, it also caused a sensual shiver to shimmer through my body. I vibrated with that bite. I had to sit down. I wanted no distractions. I needed to focus fully on the ecstasy the chocolate invoked. I took another bite, then another. And then, the truffle was gone. How could it be over so quickly? I needed more! On the tray sat several more truffles. I reached for another.

"What are you doing?" Kurt had finished his Grand Marnier truffle and raised his eyebrows at me. "You said you were going to have just one."

Kurt doesn't share my chocolate obsession and can easily be satisfied by one truffle.

"How often do you see a whole tray of Joseph Schmidt truffles in front of you? Never! This can't be coincidence. I'm going to take it as a sign that it's OK for me to eat some chocolate." I was only half joking.

When Kurt tried to interrupt, I talked over him.

"What's life about, if it can't include the pleasure of eating chocolate? You'd feel the same way if this were a giant tray of smoked salmon!" I bit into a beautiful Kahlua truffle.

Our friend's landlord overheard my last comment. "If you like chocolate, don't waste your time with this old stuff."

I stopped chewing and put the truffle down.

"That's over a week old. Come upstairs and try fresh truffles. Joseph gave them to me earlier today."

I knew I was violating my renal diet but there was no stopping me, and the promise of fresh truffles tempted Kurt to abandon his moral high ground and come along, too.

We went upstairs to the landlord's apartment, cluttered with heavy Victorian antiques, where he served us tea in bone china and a fresh batch of truffles on a filigreed silver platter. Four truffles later, I leaned back against one of the plump red velvet cushions, happy and sated, and feeling like I'd died and gone to heaven. It was only later that the guilt set in and I had to pay penance.

My phosphorus levels shot sky high. A side effect of this was that the whites of my eyes turned bright red within a week of the truffle incident. The physical evidence of my "crime" infuriated me. Whatever guilt I'd felt about violating the renal diet rules gave way to rage that my body had betrayed me and bore witness to my sin. There was nothing to do but wait. It took two weeks for my eyes to grow less red.

Though my phosphorus levels remained much higher than they should have for the year I was on PD, my food fury slowly abated. I made peace, or at least an uneasy truce, with the renal diet. I ate no more chocolate for the rest of the year I was on PD.

Cutting Back

Before getting sick, I lived at a frantic pace, continually dissatisfied that I never had enough time to do all the things I wanted. First with kidney failure, then hemodialysis, and now PD, I no longer fit my life story—the super-strong, super-fast, super-efficient, super-independent person I'd been was gone.

Everything in my life seemed to slow down. For years I'd said I'd like to have a dog or a cat, but there'd always been so many reasons not to. Now, I no longer needed to wait. I went to the pound with Marla and we found a wonderful dog that Kurt and I named Inu, on account of his being half Shiba Inu. Later, I went to the Humane Society and picked out MaxCat, an utterly fearless two-month old kitten. Inu and MaxCat added such warmth and fun to our home, it was ironic that their life with us was a direct result of my kidneys dying.

I'd hoped that once I switched to PD, I'd be able to resume working full time. During April and most of May, I managed to keep up a full schedule, but I found that by 4 p.m.

on most days, I felt fatigued and had trouble accomplishing any substantive work. By Saturday, I'd spend half the day wrapped in a wonderfully deep sleep, thanks to the morning dose of blood pressure drugs kicking in. Kurt and Cara pushed me to talk to Helen about cutting back my hours, and I finally asked her for a four-day work week. Given the wild state of the Internet economy in the middle of 1999, she was happy to have me work whatever hours I could. Fridays off gave me enough time to recover from the workweek, so that by the weekends, I had enough energy to spend quality time with Kurt.

A Change in the Tide

By May, it was becoming clear that one reason I felt so tired all the time was that I wasn't being adequately dialyzed. Kurt had been pushing me to switch doctors and medical groups, but I hadn't had the bandwidth. The PD clinic doctor had been an improvement over Dr. Pali. She never rushed our monthly PD clinic visits and patiently adjusted my medication to find a set of blood pressure drugs that worked for me, but I only saw her once a month on clinic rounds. In the interim, it was practically impossible to get her on the phone or to arrange a formal visit, what with each of our busy schedules.

Mostly, I had to rely on the PD nurse for help, but her responses to questions often frustrated me. When I asked her about the fatigue and nausea I felt after doing something no more strenuous than vacuuming, she'd say, "You're overdoing it. Relax and take it easy." I wanted to scream at her that I was only thirty-three years old, not some seventy-five year old invalid, and that less than a year before, my idea of a relaxing activity was doing a two hour flat ride instead of a four hour hilly one. She had no objective explanations for my symptoms and her casual dismissal of my complaints left me feeling powerless and depressed, so I focused on my job rather than the miserable aspects of my private life.

Kurt, however, grew impatient with the situation and took charge. He made an appointment with a primary care physician in San Francisco, who also happened to be a nephrologist. He returned with glowing reports, so I promptly scheduled a meeting with Dr. Goodman.

My first visit with Dr. Goodman underscored how different not-for-profit medical care was from that of the for-profit clinic I'd been relying on. Every meeting I'd ever had with Dr. Pali involved her speaking as fast as possible, looking at her watch, and dashing out the door after a few minutes. Dr. Goodman, on the other hand, asked me to tell him my whole story from the beginning, and he took the time to listen and ask relevant questions. Only after the secretary buzzed him for his next patient did he look at his watch, exclaiming with surprise that a whole hour had passed. He also insisted on waiving the co-pay, saying this was simply an introductory meeting. It was clear that his motives were care-driven, not profit-driven.

With Dr. Pali, it had felt like we were discussing some third party—"my condition"—rather than talking about me. The experience had been strange, alienating, and awkward. Early on, I'd noticed Dr. Pali's discomfort with emotional expression. Not wanting to appear weak or vulnerable, I'd repressed my feelings and gone along with her discursive style.

With Dr. Goodman, the experience was the complete opposite. He was a sympathetic listener. As with the time in the relaxation course when I shared with the group, I found that telling him my story provided a mirror in which I could see clearly how painful and horrific the past few months had been. I didn't want to appear hysterical or weak in our first meeting, but I broke down. Dr. Goodman was unfazed.

"It's OK to cry. You've had a really rough go of it, haven't you?" The warmth and sincerity of his smile assured me that he understood and cared. I knew I could trust him and that my well-being was a priority for him.

After our meeting, he sent me to meet Toni, the nurse in charge of the PD clinic at the San Francisco hospital where he was affiliated. She was great. She had been a nurse for twenty-five years and knew pretty much everything there was to know about peritoneal dialysis.

The first thing she did was order a KT/V, a measurement taken from a 24-hour sample of used dialysate that allowed her to calculate the percent reduction in urea I was achieving on dialysis—in other words, how well I was being dialyzed. She used this information to adjust my treatments, fine-tuning the length of my dwell times, the volume and concentration of dialysate used, and how many cycles per night to run. When I first began PD, the other PD nurse had ordered a KT/V, but she'd made few adjustments to my regimen, and I suspect she didn't understand what to do with the KT/V calculation. Toni spent all summer crunching the numbers in an effort to optimize my dialysis. As we'd learn, I was an unusually difficult case.

Babes and Babies

At my PR agency, each office had glass panels beside its door, so that even when you shut the door, people could still see into your office. From my desk, I'd spent many an odd moment looking into Kristen's office directly across the hall and marveling at how she seemed to represent the perfect example of a normal, happy and well-adjusted American woman. She'd grown up in the San Joaquin Valley on a fruit farm, a fourth or fifth generation Californian. After high school, she attended USC, where she met her husband, also descended from a long line of Californians. She was so all-American that when I used to make my afternoon chocolate runs before I got sick, even though the canteen offered an array of gourmet and organic treats, she always requested a Hershey's With Almonds chocolate bar.

Once on dialysis, I couldn't make chocolate runs, but I could still overhear her endless phone conversations with friends and her husband and wonder at her ability to integrate her personal life with work. Unlike Kristen, whenever I was at work, I felt obligated to work, and I felt guilty if anything interfered, including the demands of my body—be it dialysis or doctor visits. Kristen had married on schedule, bought a house on schedule, and on schedule, she was now pregnant with her first child.

Imagine my surprise when I came to work one Monday morning in June, and Kristen's office was silently vacant. The mystery was solved at our Monday morning staff meeting.

"Kristen had some pre-term labor over the weekend, so she's going to have to cut back her hours." Helen looked a little grim. "This means that we're all going to have to put in 110% and make sure we cover our client obligations and bill as much as possible."

Our firm was just two years old, and Kristen was our agency's first pregnancy. Everybody had been wildly excited about it, until now.

"Will Kristen be coming back?" Cara asked, once the shock died down.

"I'm sure she will, if she can. But she may have to be on bed rest the last two months of her pregnancy, so we need to be prepared to act as though she won't. We'll divvy up her clients." Helen passed out Kristen's client folders.

In the days that followed, I looked across the hall at Kristen's empty office and wondered how she was handling the disruption of her normal, on-schedule life. Did the pre-term labor throw off her good-natured equilibrium? When I received an invitation to her baby shower, I was curious to see how she was doing.

The baby shower was held in the posh East Bay suburb of Los Alamos. I left behind the cool, damp, mid-June fog of Berkeley and drove through the Caldicott Tunnel into the hot, dry inland. I turned on the air conditioner, but though I was dressed in my lightest outfit, a black floral maternity dress that didn't bind against my catheter or my abdomen, I still felt uncomfortable. Dialysis made heat intolerable. When I'd started PD, I found I couldn't comfortably wear clothes with waistbands, so I'd put my slacks and slim-fitting skirts and dresses into storage. With my swollen gut, I found maternity dresses worked best.

Unlike the small, cramped houses of my neighborhood, Los Alamos featured spreading green lawns, gracefully trimmed trees and pristine swimming pools. I parked our Toyota Corolla between a BMW and a Volvo in the spacious driveway and hurried up the curving front walk to the shady entry.

"This must be how the other half lives," I thought as I rang the doorbell.

The hostess answered the door, her blond hair tastefully short and makeup immaculate. As I stepped into the sunken living room, I felt as though I'd entered a movie set or perhaps a page from a California good living magazine like Sunset. Everything matched, the Seventies architecture updated with Nineties interior design. From the cream-colored curtains and the white Berber carpet to the sky blue throw pillows on the overstuffed couches and the ivory placemats on the dining room table, the place was picture perfect.

Slim women dressed in summer-light designer casual wear lounged demurely about, sipping lemonade and exchanging pleasantries. I felt like some huge black thing, ugly and out of place, parodying pregnancy in my maternity dress, my gut swollen not with a baby but with the visual proof of my disease. I lumbered over to Kristen, who sat radiantly large on one of the couches.

"Hi, Lisa. I'm glad you could make it," she smiled and looked down at my gut. "How're you doing?"

What could I say? I didn't want to be the big black cloud. Surrounded by such beauty and perfection, there was nothing to do but lie. I smiled back at her.

"Just fine, Kristen. How are you?"

Everyone gathered around to listen to her story, chuckling at the funny parts, clucking sympathetically at the sad ones, and above all witnessing the confident glow of impending motherhood that emanated from her. Bed rest had not shaken her serene equilibrium.

As she talked about sonograms and visits to the doctor, I found myself remembering the previous summer. Like Kristen's, my life had seemed on track. I had the husband, we'd bought the house, I'd started the new job. We were going to start a family. But, instead of a kid, I ended up with dead kidneys.

Here I sat, a sappy smile stuck on my face, surrounded by beautiful babes contemplating babies. Was I sad? Resentful? Envious? Jealous? Angry? All these emotions flooded through me while I sipped the lemonade and picked at what little I could eat of the non-renal-friendly lunch menu.

After the baby shower, I found myself thinking about having a baby. I searched online to discover what research had been conducted on PD pregnancy, but it was scant and critical. Regardless, I continued to think about babies.

In my darkest moments, I cried not for the loss of my kidneys but for the lost chance of a child. It seemed somehow easier to mourn this loss than my dead kidneys and the loss of the self I had been. I felt a sweet simple sadness when I imagined a baby, perfect and pure, who'd never be, but when I thought of my own demise, the feelings weren't sweet nor simple. There was sadness, true, but there was also rage, shame, and guilt, as well as frustration, jealousy and impatience. Though Kurt tried to reassure me that I'd most likely be able to have a child after the transplant, I wasn't ready to think about the future. I still had to survive the present.

Sustaining My Strength

By June, I struggled to sustain what was left of my physical fitness after six months on dialysis. Before getting sick, I'd been a hard core cyclist as well as a trail runner and hiker, once referred to as "the Blonde Amazon" by a friend, but now my kidneys no longer manufactured erythropoietin, the hormone responsible for telling my bone marrow to generate new red blood cells. Anemia stole my strength. Early in my PD treatment, I'd been prescribed weekly injections of Epogen, an artificial equivalent to erythropoietin, to help boost my hematocrit, the measurement of my red blood cells. As soon as I switched clinics, Toni immediately upped the dose. By June, I was injecting Epo into the fat above the muscle on my thigh several times a week.

When I first brought home the little glass bottles of Epo, Kurt joked that I should save some for him. Epo is a favorite drug among elite cyclists for boosting their performance. As soon as he saw the disposable syringes, however, he blanched. Hypodermic needles terrified him. I didn't like getting shots either, but this was something I had to learn to do, or else I'd be forced to drive to the clinic to get the shots.

The secret I found for injecting myself was to not completely focus on what I was doing. Sure, I paid attention to procedure, using a new disposable syringe each time and wiping my thigh with a fresh alcohol pad, but when it came time for the actual shot, I didn't pause to think about what I was doing. If I paused, I'd risk losing the courage to stick myself, so instead, I'd quickly thrust the needle in, smoothly depress the plunger, and swiftly pull the needle out. I learned from experience that you wanted the process to be quick.

Epo increased my energy, but there was no way I could return to even a small approximation of my former fitness. One day in June I tried to ride what had been an easy twenty-minute commute to work six months before. Though the ride in wasn't so bad since it was mainly downhill, and I always felt better in the mornings after the ten-hour nightly dialysis, I almost didn't make it home that evening. My legs became useless leaden weights, my heart throbbed painfully as if threatening a heart attack, and my stomach churned with heartburn and nausea. Defeated, I drove to work from then on.

Unable to bike for exercise, I tried jogging, but the dialysate proved an insurmountable problem. During physical exertion, my diaphragm inflated from heavy breathing and my body jiggled up and down. This, combined with the two-plus liters of dialysate in my gut, pushed my diaphragm up against my stomach and esophagus, triggering painful heartburn and nausea. I tried draining the dialysate and exercising "dry," but I still couldn't summon the energy in my legs needed to jog.

Fortunately, I was still strong enough to walk. So that summer, I walked every night after work. I ventured uphill from our house and discovered an extensive network of footpaths winding through the Berkeley hills, paths I'd never seen when I was healthy and speeding about on my bike. The stair-step paths were too steep to run and impossible to bike, and I relished the fact that I was pursuing a physical activity I'd never done when healthy. Small compensation, but enough. The walks strengthened me sufficiently so that over the summer I was able to walk the high elevation trails of the Sierra without too much struggle.

Role Reversal

By the Fourth of July, Kurt and I needed a vacation. We arranged a trip to Mineral King in southern Sequoia National Park, where we'd held our wedding celebration in 1996, the year before we left our academic lives in Pennsylvania to join the Internet boom in the Bay Area. We hadn't been back since then.

Evan, Kurt's friend since junior high in Indiana was staying with us for a few weeks while he waited for his summer job to start in Colorado. Working the Beaver Creek ski season in winter and leading outdoor adventure tours in summer, Evan had made a life for himself as a professional outdoors enthusiast. While the guys excitedly planned their hiking itinerary, I packed the two-liter bags of dialysate and other supplies I'd need for gravity PD. The campground didn't have power, so I wouldn't be able to use the cycler.

We left first thing Saturday morning, and by early afternoon we drove the torturous twenty-five mile Mineral King road, winding up the six-thousand-foot climb. The road twisted past chaparral and granite outcroppings, the sun searing down with the fiery intensity of early July in the Sierra foothills, the scent of sage and pine resin in the air. Then, around a tight bend in the road, we abruptly encountered the massive, red-barked base of the first giant sequoia. Kurt carefully maneuvered the Toyota on the single-lane road where it detoured around the tree. He switched on Vivaldi's Four Seasons, which soared statically over the Toyota's lousy speakers.

"We always listen to the Four Seasons when we get to the sequoias." Kurt spoke over his shoulder to Evan, who sat in the back seat with Inu, who lay panting across his lap. "It seems a fitting tribute."

As always, the sequoias awed me, their massive magnificence and monumental age, some well over a thousand years old. Our lives, my physical woes, seemed insignificant.

I tried to keep this in mind when we arrived at Atwell Mills and began to set up camp, but I was having trouble. I wasn't prepared for the shock, the juxtaposition of my current physical state with the memories of how strong and gloriously energetic I'd been, before. Everywhere I looked reminded me of my last trip here, three years earlier, when I'd been in peak condition.

Now, I sat in the car performing my afternoon exchange and watched Evan and Kurt move about the camp. Though Evan was joking, I noticed Kurt seemed unusually somber. He didn't say anything about it, so when they left for a quick hike before our other friends showed up, I didn't bother asking him what was going on.

Instead, I escaped the gnats by hiding in the tent and trying to take a nap. As soon as I lay down, however, the racking coughs fired up, so instead, I sat at the campsite picnic table, swatted at flies, and felt sorry for myself until our Southern California friends arrived. They'd all visited me over the holidays when I first began hemodialysis, but we hadn't seen each other since. While they set up their tents, I described my life on PD to them.

When Kurt and Evan got back, I was shocked at how pale, almost yellow, Kurt looked. I took him aside.

"Are you feeling OK?"

"I've got this pain in my gut. I thought it might've been indigestion, but it's getting worse." He grimaced and squeezed his hand against his lower left abdomen. "Don't say anything to anyone yet. Maybe it'll go away." He walked over to the picnic table and sat down.

It was obvious that he didn't want to call off the vacation we'd both so looked forward to and that he didn't want to worry the others, especially if it was nothing.

But what if it was something, like appendicitis? I couldn't remember which side the appendix was on, but one thing was certain: it would be a hellaciously long two-hour drive back down the steep Mineral King road in an emergency. I knew he was thinking this, too, but short of ordering him down the mountain, there was nothing I could do. I had to wait for him to either feel better or drop his stoic behavior.

Everybody worked to get dinner ready, but I kept a surreptitious eye on Kurt, who was looking even worse, his color sliding from yellow to green. He suddenly looked old.

"Are you sure you don't want to leave?" I asked as we prepared for bed.

"Let's just wait a little longer and see if it mellows out."

Our night was miserable. I don't know if it was the elevation or the jiggling from our drive up the bumpy road, but my coughing reached new, orchestral heights. A small cough would sneak out, I'd try to squelch it, worried about waking our friends in the neighboring tents, but the little cough would unleash a growing chorus of coughs, louder, more guttural and phlegmatic, until a ferocious echoing hack would free bloody snot from my nose. Then, sucking frantically on a cough drop, I'd wait shakily for respite. Meanwhile, Kurt tossed restlessly from side to side. Finally, at 4 a.m., his voice came to me out of the darkness.

"We've gotta go. Something's really wrong. I've got to get to ER."

It was so dark we could barely make out where Evan lay sleeping in the nearby meadow. Kurt woke him and relayed the news. I managed to find another friend in the darkness and whispered that we had to leave.

"What are you going to do?" she whispered back.

"I guess we have to find the nearest hospital."

The trip down the mountain was not the relaxed outing of the day before. The road demanded 100% of my attention as I drove as fast as I could without killing us, which on that road was barely more than 15 mph. Evan and Inu were silent in the back seat, probably asleep, while Kurt sat rigidly beside me, his lips set in a grim line.

"How are you doing?" I asked after a while.

"It hurts, but it's not getting any worse. Maybe we can make it home." Kurt still looked yellow, but perhaps not quite so green.

"I don't know if that's a good idea. What if it's an appendicitis? What if it's something worse?" I couldn't help thinking that maybe Murphy's Law had returned, now threatening Kurt.

"I'd like to avoid the hospital if we can," he insisted.

The sun rose as we reached the bottom of the Mineral King road. The ranger at the Park entrance turned out to be a retired nurse.

"You say it's on your left side? Well, then it's definitely not your appendix."

"I guess we can drive home," Kurt said hopefully.

"No, sir. I would not recommend that. You don't want to mess around with abdominal pain that lasts for more than a few hours."

The nurse turned to me. "Why don't you drive him down to the hospital in Visalia. It's the closest, and the drive should only take you about an hour and a half."

Her words spooked us. After all, she'd been a nurse and seemed to know what she was talking about. Rather than second-guess her, we descended into San Joaquin Valley's scorching heat in search of help.

The hospital was shockingly cold and dark after the bright light intensity of the Visalia streets. Kurt and I sat in the ER waiting room while Evan dog-sat Inu somewhere outside. Unlike the ER in Berkeley, this one was completely vacant except for us. Were there fewer casualties in the more rural Visalia? Or, was 9 o'clock on a Saturday morning a good time to be in ER?

I couldn't believe we were back in the hospital, but now Kurt was the sick one. We waited in silence. I leafed through an outdated issue of Newsweek while Kurt sat with his eyes closed, his mouth tight.

Before long, a young, slightly overweight doctor hurried over and greeted us with a grin. We immediately noticed his tie. It was loudly multicolored and made of rubber. He caught us staring at it.

"Yep, it's rubber all right. Isn't it a blast?" He chuckled.

Kurt and I didn't.

"You must be Kurt," the doctor continued. "Come and let's have a look at you." He turned to me. "We may have to run a few tests if I can't immediately find out what's wrong, so this could take a little while."

He seemed competent, if a little eccentric, but who can tell from such a brief interaction? We didn't have a choice in selecting the doctor, not if Kurt wanted to be seen as soon as possible.

So I waited, and waited. Memories of my own hospital visits flooded through me and my emotions warred against each other: frustration that our vacation had been cut off, fury at being be back in the hospital yet again, but mainly, fear for Kurt. I hoped someone would tell me something before I had to leave for my afternoon dialysis in the boiling hot car. Three hours later, a wholesome-looking young nurse approached.

"We've put Kurt in a room since we're still waiting on some test results. I'll take you to him."

On the fifth floor, his room had an excellent view (if you can call it that) of Visalia. He gave me a big smile when I walked in.

"Hi, there. They gave me some drugs to stop the pain."

DIALYSIS: A MEMOIR

I sat beside him on the bed and kissed him. Though he looked perfectly fine now, no longer yellow-green, I wasn't prepared to see him in a hospital gown. This one, unlike the plain blue ones at the Berkeley hospital, had an intricate pastel floral design on it, which on Kurt looked incongruous. When he walked over to the window to point out the view, his legs poked out from under the gown, looking more bony than muscular. Kurt was Mr. Mountain man, khakis and natural earth tones and adventure gear. The pastel gown, besides looking silly, made him seem frail, delicate, and vulnerable.

I didn't like seeing him this way. I needed to think of him as the strong one, as the one who could handle any physical or emotional challenge. I tried to reassure myself that the acute onset of his symptoms probably meant that whatever was going on wasn't too serious. As I'd learned, it was those slow creeping problems that were the truly dangerous ones.

We reclined on the bed and watched cable TV while we waited for the doctor. Neither of us was prepared for what he had to say when he came in, about an hour later.

"I'm afraid we're going to have to operate." He looked grave, the comical rubber tie now clashing with his somber expression.

"What?!" we exclaimed.

He hurried to explain that none of the tests had been definitive and that Kurt could be suffering from one of two possibilities.

"In the first case, we wouldn't need to do anything. But if you've got an intestinal rupture, we need to get in there and fix it as soon as possible."

He explained that if this were the case, Kurt ran a serious risk of infection, perhaps even death, and the only way to definitively rule out this possibility was to go in, surgically, and take a look.

We stared at him in disbelief. Abruptly, Kurt shook his head.

"No, Doctor. I do not want surgery. In fact, I feel fine and I would like to leave now."

The doctor was shocked. "I don't advise that."

"What are you thinking?" I whispered to Kurt, worried that his prejudice and fear of doctors might be influencing his decision.

"Before deciding on surgery, I want to drive back to Berkeley and see my own doctor."

"I've already spoken to your doctor, and he's agreed with my assessment." The doctor sounded a little obstinate.

"I want to speak to him," Kurt demanded.

"Sure, OK. Let me get his phone number." The doctor left the room.

I turned to Kurt and repeated my question. "What are you thinking?"

"I don't trust his diagnosis. I feel totally fine now, and I don't believe there's any reason for me to undergo surgery. I think the sooner we get out of here the better." He was adamant. "These country doctors! For all we know, he's probably out to make a buck, recommending surgery just like that. I want to know what Dr. Goodman thinks."

Surprisingly, Dr. Goodman backed the doctor. If Kurt wouldn't agree to the exploratory surgery, then Dr. Goodman agreed that Kurt should remain under observation for the next twenty-four hours.

After Kurt's call, the doctor prepared to leave. "If your condition hasn't deteriorated tomorrow, then it'll probably be OK for you to risk driving to the Bay Area." He tucked Kurt's chart under his arm. "But you need to promise me that the first thing you do when you get there is see Dr. Goodman for an examination."

"Sure thing," Kurt said as he left the room.

I knew immediately from Kurt's tone that he had no intention of doing that. Unlike me, he didn't feel compelled to play the compliant patient.

When the doctor left, he asked, "Where are Evan and Inu?"

"I'm not sure. I left them out in the parking lot behind the hospital when we came in. I guess I'd better go find them and tell Evan we'll have to get a hotel room. I've also gotta do an exchange."

Unfortunately, all pet-friendly hotels in town were booked for the 4th of July weekend, which meant that Evan and I spent the afternoon and evening trading off duties, either dog-sitting Inu or visiting Kurt. By that night, we had an intimate knowledge of Visalia's hot asphalt streets, all seventy-one cable channels on the hotel and hospital TVs, and of the absolute necessity of air conditioning in the San Joaquin Valley. By the next morning, we were desperate to get out of there. Kurt felt fine and refused to wait the full twenty-four hours. Instead, we left bright and early and as soon as he could fill out the paperwork.

"We are releasing you against the doctor's orders." The nurse frowned at Kurt. "We can't be held responsible for your well-being once we release you."

"Yeah, yeah." Kurt hurried me out to the car, where Evan and Inu waited.

As we drove back across the Valley, the Toyota's air conditioning was thankfully strong enough to handle the early morning heat. Kurt yawned widely.

"I'm tired. Last night sucked! I can't believe how many times they came in to poke and prod me."

He leaned back in the passenger seat and reached over to run his hand under the hair lying against my neck, letting the cool air circulate. I was sad our holiday weekend had been no vacation, but I was grateful he was OK. I leaned back into his hand, enjoying his touch and thankful that our role reversal had come to an end.

He finally did go and see Dr. Goodman for a checkup, though the doctor didn't find anything wrong. It wasn't until years later that he was diagnosed with diverticulitis—but that's a whole other story.

Work Woes

Helen ran our boutique PR agency with a controlled yet relaxed hand. She divided the clients among the seven of us in such a way that we each owned at least one account and provided back up on at least one other, and none of us worked more than three accounts at a time. Though she met with each team's leader once a week to make sure she was aware of the clients' activities, she allowed the teams to run themselves. Since this was only my second PR job, she initially gave me a small account to lead, and I provided back up on the enormous BoldVision account led by Cara.

This arrangement worked well, even once I got sick. My client rarely required more than an occasional press release or media call, so I focused primarily on helping Cara. Together, she and I became BoldVision's lean mean PR machine. She was "Miss Smile-and-Dial," charming the reporters and winning their interest, and I was "The Executor," "The Spam Queen," crafting pithy pitches, whipping out press releases, and emailing all relevant contacts around the globe. Our teamwork grew beyond her simply being the charm and me the brains. We had fun working together, and we became friends.

Once when we sent out a press release that required a hellacious call-down (we had to call all two hundred and fifty people on the contact list) and I was doing my 2:30 p.m. exchange, she called me on the speaker phone, laughing.

"Why I'm just bumping my gums over here calling all these people, while you're over there doing the dialysis disco!" She had a turn of phrase that could make me smile even when I was harried or in a morbid state of mind.

In our roles as the charm and the brains, Cara met with Helen and the client, whereas I flew pretty much under the radar. Cara shielded my sickness from the client, and from Helen. This all changed one day in July, when Cara came into my office and closed the door.

"Lisa, I haven't told anyone this yet, but I'm leaving." She spoke softly to avoid being overheard. "It's too good an opportunity to turn down. I'll be Director of Corporate Communications, and they're offering me a huge stack of pre

IPO stock." She paused, then dropped the drama to speak candidly and with concern. "Are you going to be OK when I'm gone?"

"Sure, I'll be fine," I said, not sure I was telling the truth.

She looked so happy, so excited. I hadn't yet thought through the implications of her leaving.

I don't know the whole story, but she left under a dark cloud that rocked the agency for months afterwards. She gave her two weeks notice on Friday, but when she showed up the following Monday morning for our staff meeting, Helen shocked us all. As Cara moved to sit down among the rest of us, Helen's face broke its usual studied composure.

"Get out," she scowled at Cara and pointed to the door.

We all turned to look at Cara, who stood motionless, her face bright red.

"What?" She finally broke the disturbing silence.

"I said, get out. Now." Helen rose to her feet, her voice shaking with rage.

Cara moved toward her office.

"No!" Helen stepped between Cara and her office door. "Leave, now."

"But what about my stuff?"

"Get out."

Cara's face went from red to white. "I'm just going to get my purse." She ran past Helen into her office. Seconds later, the door to the agency slammed shut behind her.

Once Cara disappeared, Helen regained her poise, and the rest of the staff meeting proceeded as usual, at least as far as Helen's behavior. The rest of us stared at her in stunned silence. What had led to such an outburst?

Something changed at the agency after that day, a certain fear now circulated among us about Helen. I had the feeling there must have been more to the story about Cara's leaving, which would have explained Helen's outburst, but I was an outsider to their personal relationship.

The day after Helen walked Cara out, my own world at the agency turned upside down. First, Helen called me into her spacious corner office.

"What do you think about taking over the BoldVision account?" She gazed at me across her vast mahogany desk.

"Me? But don't you think my being on dialysis is a problem?" I was surprised. I'd known she'd need to reorganize the account, but it hadn't occurred to me that she'd consider me as Cara's replacement.

"You're the best prepared to tackle the account, Lisa," she said.

She didn't go on. Instead, we sat silently for some time. Helen had mastered the art of sitting in silence, leaving the other person to squirm and eventually reveal whatever information they had. I am sure this strategy played a key role in her gleaning crucial information for winning accounts and controlling uppity clients. She was not given to idle chitchat.

I broke her gaze and stared blindly out the window. I thought about all the pros and cons of taking the account. With its stock at an all-time high, new product launches practically every month, and a burgeoning list of satisfied clients, BoldVision was soaring high, an Internet superstar the press was eating up, and the job would be tremendously exciting. It would also be an enormous promotion.

And yet, the stress would be proportional. I was exhausted with my current job duties, though Helen probably didn't know how much. As I sat there thinking, I knew she wanted me to take the account. It would make things easier for her in terms of staffing and training, and saying no would mean letting her down, but then I thought of those late night trips to ER, the various surgeries. If I ran such a demanding account, I'd no longer have Fridays off.

"I can't do it, Helen. I'm sorry." I finally met her gaze and tried to put the best spin on it. "BoldVision needs someone who can be available twenty-four-seven. With my medical situation, I can't guarantee something won't come up."

Helen responded without blinking an eye. "How about you stay on the account and report to Rochelle." It was not a question. "You'll have to help her get up to speed, but that shouldn't take more than a few weeks."

I agreed to her proposal and, as I left her office, I wondered disconcertedly if she'd planned the interview to end exactly as it did. Had she actually thought I was physically capable of leading the BoldVision account? Or, had she asked simply as a means of forcing me to reject taking the account? I could see how she'd acquired her reputation as a master strategist. It was impossible to read what she thought of my illness, since she offered no indication, verbal or otherwise.

Where Cara had been a bundle of laughs and spontaneous voluptuous humor, Rochelle was all angles and boundaries, sharp edges. Rochelle commuted from Marin rather than live near work, and she radiated a Marin-like aura, her clothes beautifully and expensively understated in all-natural fibers. She had a penchant for pale blues and whites, perhaps to accentuate her blue eyes, and she only wore silver jewelry. The latest excitement in her life was upgrading from a Saab convertible to a white Volvo sedan. She was also a firm believer in Franklin Planners and, within a week of coming on board the BoldVision account, had signed me up for my own planner.

"You need to plan, organize and prioritize." She lectured me repeatedly during our frequent meetings. "Tracking and accounting are absolutely necessary. The clients need to know exactly how their money is being spent." She arched her perfectly plucked eyebrows in consternation. "I have just got to clean up these reports!"

When Cara and I had worked together, we spent most of our time publicizing BoldVision. With Rochelle, the focus became administrative reporting. Without Cara as my sounding board and compatriot, I found pitching lost much of its fun, but I continued to pitch as much as possible because now there was only one of us doing the publicity.

Ironically, the more Rochelle stressed accounting, the more I found myself losing track of my action items and forgetting to do things. My memory wasn't improved by my pervasive, continual fatigue. Codeine cough syrup for the coughing and antihistamines for the allergies helped me sleep, but I never awoke refreshed. There was so much I had to remember about everything, from the requirements of my dialysis—my diet, the schedule, the protocol—to all the action items of my job.

The situation exploded in early August, when Helen called me into her office first thing Monday morning.

"Where's the BoldVision story in the Merc?" She had the San Jose Mercury News website up on her computer and scrolled down the screen, pointing at the headlines.

"I don't know. It should be there." I was sure the reporter had run the story.

"Well, it's not. Jane has already called twice asking for it, so you had better find out why, Lisa."

I hurried back to my office, a cold fear gripping my heart. Jane was the PR Manager at BoldVision and, if she had already called Helen about the story first thing on a Monday morning, then it must mean BoldVision's CEO was looking for the coverage. I vaguely waved "Good Morning" to Rochelle as I rushed by her office, then closed the door and hid in my office. I had to find out what had happened before anyone else heard about it.

I pulled up my email, pulled out my phone log, and tried to reconstruct events of the previous Thursday, my last day at work. I remembered receiving the working draft of the press release from Jane to use for pitching the press, and I remembered pitching the reporter and offering her an exclusive, since the Merc was BoldVision's top media target for this particular story.

As far as I could remember, I'd faxed the finalized copy of the press release to the reporter at the end of the day, when I finally got the approved version from BoldVision. Unlike some reporters, this reporter was both diligent and cautious.

She wouldn't run the news unless she knew it had been signed off on by BoldVision and their legal team. For the life of me, I couldn't remember not faxing it. But then I also remembered Wednesday night had been particularly rough. My coughing spasms following the first fill cycle on the dialysis machine had led to my vomiting up most of my dinner, and I'd had to resort to codeine cough syrup to soothe my throat in order to sleep. Thursday, I'd been exhausted.

I sent the reporter an email and even left her voicemail, something I rarely did because reporters often viewed this as PR harassment. In the meantime, I frantically busied myself with all the other publicity activities of the day, hoping I'd hear back from the reporter before Rochelle got wind of the situation and BroadVision's CEO leaned on Jane for the news. Finally, a curt email arrived from the reporter.

"You did not send me the final press release, so I could not run the story."

How could that be? I must have sent it. I wouldn't have forgotten to do something so important, would I? Before I had any more chance to think, Helen buzzed me into her office.

"Well, what can I tell BoldVision? Where's the story?" She gave me the same deadpan look she always did, but it didn't help me feel better. I wished I could lie, anything rather than admit my failure, but that was impossible. I had to tell her the truth.

"I'm sorry, but I guess I screwed up. Apparently, I didn't fax the Merc the finalized press release last week."

I'd vowed to maintain a professional front with Helen, mistress of the poker face. As it was, I failed miserably at that, as well. I couldn't stop the tears.

"You've put me in a difficult position, Lisa. We promised this story to BoldVision, and now I've got to account for why the Merc didn't run it. I'm sure you can understand how awkward this is."

She looked at me, her face still expressionless. I grabbed a tissue from her desk.

"I know, I'm sorry." I knew she hated apologies, but I couldn't stop the words.

"Make sure this doesn't happen again." She waved me out of the office, but then added, "I'll take care of the situation."

"How?" I asked at the door.

Her expression altered subtly. "I'll lie."

Once back in the relative privacy of my office, I shut the door and fell apart. I'd prided myself at being good at my job, and most days, it was the drive to do my job that got me out of bed, unhooked from the dialysis machine, and out of the house. Working with Cara had played a vital role in helping me feel like I could succeed at something after my kidneys failed, and her vivacious spirit had helped offset my suffering.

When she left, I thought I could absorb many of her duties into the ones I was already performing and still succeed. I thought I could avoid missing her by keeping busy, and maybe, vainly, I also wanted to be PR superwoman.

Eventually, I pulled myself together and the crisis at work blew over. But the experience left me with questions: Was my increasing forgetfulness a rebellion against Rochelle's obsession with accounting? Or was it the result of extreme fatigue (I hadn't had a good night's sleep in months)? Or, was it a side effect of one of the many drugs I was on? Most likely it was a combination of all these things, but I was soon to learn that my forgetfulness could have life-threatening consequences.

Chapter 8 - On the Road

Traveling on PD

Travel has always played an important part of my relationship with Kurt. Since we first met in graduate school, we spent every summer camping, backpacking, and mountain biking, either in the Sierra or the Rockies, and we prided ourselves on our self-sufficiency and ability to survive in the rugged natural world. Before my illness, I'd been a physical match for Kurt, not only traveling with him to these spectacular outdoor locations but also accompanying him on strenuous adventures, bagging peaks, mountain biking over thirteen-thousand-foot passes, and backpacking the high Sierra.

Traveling on dialysis wasn't impossible. For camping and car trips, I simply had to pack my PD supplies in the car and off we went, though without the cycler, I had to perform four extra gravity exchanges each day in addition to my usual afternoon exchange. Travel by plane was even easier. All I had to do was call the dialysis company, let them know my travel dates, where I would be staying, and what amount and concentration of dialysate I'd need. They shipped all the boxes, free of charge. The only difficulty was that I had to lug the dialysis machine with me on the plane. During the time I was on PD, I took one plane trip to Los Angeles and, except for tweaking my lower back hoisting the machine into the overhead bin, I found plane travel not too difficult. Car trips to the mountains were another story.

In the high Sierra, the most I could manage were laboriously slow walks up trails I'd previously run, breathing hard and struggling to overcome the nausea rising from the dialysate jiggling in my gut, the trembling weakness in my legs threatening to obliterate the memories of their once surging strength. The only thing that surged now was my blood pressure when I spent nights above four thousand feet. I also discovered that at higher elevations I developed severe water retention, which meant having to increase the dialysate concentration.

Rather than abandon our summer trips, we modified how we did them. We'd spend nights at cheap motels in the lower elevation town of Bishop in the Owens Valley and take day trips up to the high Sierra. This way Kurt could continue bagging his peaks and I could at least enjoy the fresh mountain air and see some of the sights.

But it also meant we spent the time apart. Over the summer, Kurt invited other friends to join him on his mountain climbs while I found myself plodding up the trails alone. I spent some of the time in meditation, and I enjoyed the fact that moving slowly meant I could take the time to fully appreciate the intricate beauty of nature rather than race through it toward some distant peak. At the same time, however, I also felt a gulf growing between other people and me. My life now seemed so different from "normal" people's lives. Even something as simple as going to sleep, which had once been the trivial act of sliding into bed, now entailed preparation, supplies, and machinery. Forgetting this could kill me.

The Importance of Second Checks

Over the summer, two trips to the Sierra underscored the importance of second checks. On the first trip, Kurt's cousin joined us. We drove across the San Joaquin Valley on a Friday night after work and arrived at 11 p.m. in Groveland, a small town just outside Yosemite National Park.

After checking in and lugging our bags to the hotel room, we all looked forward to sleep. I immediately set up the cycler, but when I went to prime the machine, I discovered I'd forgotten the cassettes.

"How could I have forgotten them?" I repeated over and over, in complete disbelief. I was sure I'd packed them, but they weren't there.

"We've got to drive back to Berkeley and get them," Kurt sighed.

"I could go alone." I didn't want him to lose sleep over my mistake.

"Don't be ridiculous. I'll come, but you'll have to drive the first stretch, since I drove us here." He looked at his cousin. "Inu will have to stay with you." Poor Inu lay on one of the beds, looking only slightly less car sick now that he was on stable ground. Unlike most dogs, Inu hated car rides.

Kurt's cousin agreed and we hurried out the door, anxious to get the drive underway.

Since I was missing my dialysis time, I hooked myself up to one of the two-liter bags and began an exchange while we drove back across the Valley. The dialysate drained into the bag at my feet, and I set my timer for twenty minutes to remind me when I should begin filling.

I drove fast, hoping to make good time. The dark road swept away before us, a limitless, unimpeded stretch of space, the routinely heavy foothills traffic absent at this late hour. I watched the speedometer inch higher and I thrilled at the power of the rental's V-6. As our speed increased to over one hundred miles per hour, the exhilaration I felt contained a curious combination of joy and rage.

Here was something fast and daring that even a dialysis patient could do. No kidneys needed for this! But what of the risk? A deer could jump out in front of us, or we could get a blowout. A small part of me felt there was nothing to lose. Faster and faster we flew. Suddenly, a single pair of headlights appeared on the dark road behind us. Another speeder? A cop? I eased off. My heart began to race.

"I think a cop just nailed me." I couldn't pull my eyes away from the rearview mirror.

"How fast were you going?" Kurt struggled awake.

"I don't know. Maybe a hundred?" I lied. It had been faster. In the rearview mirror, I saw the car light up like a Christmas tree. I pulled over.

"You could tell him that you've got a medical emergency and that's why you were driving so fast." Kurt thought through the possible ways to avoid a ticket.

"No. That could totally backfire. He might say we have to go to a hospital or something, and I don't think he'd approve of us driving across the valley in the middle of the night while I'm dialyzing. I hope he doesn't see the drain bag. What if he asks me to get out of the car?" I pushed the drain bag under the driver's seat once we stopped. The fill bag sat in its warmer on the backseat.

Fortunately, the policeman approached the car on the passenger side. After briefly shining his flashlight on both of our faces (probably to check if we were drunk), he conducted the interview in the dark.

"Do you know how fast you were driving back there—" he looked at my license, "Lisa?"

I took the innocent approach. "No, Officer."

"Well, I clocked you at seventy-eight miles per hour."

"Really? I guess I wasn't paying attention." I fought to keep from smiling in gratitude that he hadn't caught my real speed, or at least wasn't citing me for anything close to it. I was doubly grateful that he hadn't noticed the tube attached to me and the full bag of yellow liquid rolling around on the car floor. I dutifully signed for my first and only speeding ticket, and I swore to Kurt that I'd never forget my supplies again.

"Next time, make a list of your supplies and check it before we leave." Kurt didn't spend time complaining or blaming me for our late night journey across the valley, and I again felt grateful.

"Of course," I answered.

Famous last words.

Toward the end of July, we took another trip to the mountains, this time to the Western slope. We were planning to explore the area around the American River north of Placerville. When it came time for my afternoon exchange, we pulled over by the side of a remote mountain road. I sent Kurt and Inu off for a half-hour walk while I sat in the driver's seat and hooked up to a two-liter bag.

I got as far as completing the exchange, when I suddenly realized I'd forgotten the disposable caps I needed to seal my catheter. I couldn't disconnect! How could I have been so stupid? Again and again, I replayed in my head those moments I'd spent packing. I couldn't believe I'd forgotten something so basic as the caps. But the worst of it was that, even though I'd written out a checklist as Kurt had recommended, I still hadn't actually conducted a second check.

"I've got some bad news," I told him when he came back with Inu. "I can't disconnect. I forgot the caps."

"You what?! How could you have forgotten them? Didn't you do a second check?" He put Inu in the back and sat down on the passenger seat, completely exasperated.

"I'm sorry." I cringed, red with shame and embarrassment. I'd screwed up, again. "I didn't do a second check because I knew I had everything. I thought I did."

Silence.

"Well, you were wrong." He folded his arms across his chest and glared at me.

"I guess there's nothing to do but drive back home and get the caps," I sighed.

"I'm not spending another vacation doing all that driving across the fucking valley, OK? I spent the last two weekends working and this was supposed to be our vacation!"

"I know, I'm sorry. But what can we do?"

"Let's drive back down to Placerville. Maybe we can find some caps there."

With the bags still attached to me, I drove back to Placerville. While Kurt went in search of caps, I sat in the car and waited, hoping we could salvage the situation.

The volunteer at the Placerville Visitor's Center had been a nurse for thirty years and offered to help Kurt. She first called the regional hospital, which referred her to the local PD clinic. Unfortunately, it being Saturday, the clinic was closed.

We were out of luck. There was nothing to do but drive home. Our vacation was ruined.

These two experiences made me painfully aware of the importance of "second checks." At the hemodialysis clinic, the nurses and their assistants had always reviewed all the lines and equipment a second time to make sure everything was OK before hooking up their patients. After all, their patients' lives were literally in their hands. While at home and surrounded by a plethora of PD supplies, it hadn't occurred to me that I might travel to places where without those supplies I could die. These were places I had visited freely since childhood, but now simply being there without PD supplies endangered my life.

Birthday Blessings

For my birthday in August, Kurt made reservations at a pro-dog, environmentally friendly resort in Mendocino County. The place advertised individual secluded cabins, each uniquely designed, each solar-powered, and each situated out of sight from the others. I was skeptical.

"'Mule Dung Ranch'? That doesn't sound very appealing." And then it occurred to me. "Hey, if the cabins are solar-powered, do they have outlets? Do you think they have enough energy to run the cycler?"

Kurt made the requisite calls. As it turned out, none of the solar-powered cabins had enough power, but fortunately, the guest cabin adjacent to the main house shared its power grid. We'd have less privacy, but I'd be able to use the cycler.

We arrived so late on Friday night that I had to immediately hook up. The next morning, we explored the ranch. I saw neither mule nor dung and the place was remarkably beautiful. Kurt took Inu for a run while I found a grassy knoll that faced west with a panoramic view of the giant green Mendocino coastal range.

I sat and reflected on turning thirty-four and the year that had passed. Though grateful to be alive, I wondered what my life might have been like if I hadn't gotten sick. We probably would have had a kid by now, but instead, no kidneys. Walking back to the cabin, I tried to focus my attention on the beauty of the poppies and the lupine and not feel bitter.

Later, after Kurt showered and we packed up the car, we walked over to the main house to inquire about the check-out procedure. The building was gorgeous, with large wood beams and gigantic windows optimizing the sweeping western vista. A man came out of the house and greeted us.

"You must be Kurt and Lisa. I'm Paul." He looked to be in his early thirties and wore a blue baseball cap over his short, blond hair. "David told me about your situation. I'm sorry to hear you're sick." He smiled at me. The blue cap perfectly matched the color of his eyes.

"It's not so bad." I tried to shrug off his concern. "Who's David?"

Peter explained that David was his uncle and the owner of Mule Dung Ranch. He gave us a little of the place's history.

"There were mules here at one time, back fifty years or so. David bought the land about ten years ago and has been slowly building up the place."

"Do you work here? What a wonderful place to live," I enthused, writing out the check to pay for our night's stay.

Paul nodded. "I count my blessings that David and Jessica have let me stay on."

"We're glad we can help you, Paul, in whatever way we can." A spry, older woman came down from the main house to join us by our car. "He's doing a lot better than when he first got here." Jessica smiled confidentially at us.

"This is my aunt, Jessica. She's been worried because I have HIV," Paul explained.

My brain spun in shock. Paul had HIV? But he had just given me sympathy about my dead kidneys! I couldn't believe it. I tuned back in to what he was saying to Jessica.

"This is the young woman I was telling you about. She's had kidney failure and is on dialysis. That's why they needed to rent the guest house—for her dialysis machine."

"Oh my," Jessica exclaimed. "I hope you had a good stay."

"We did. You have a great place," Kurt said.

While he and Jessica discussed the unique architecture of the buildings, I approached Paul. I had to know more about his condition. "You have HIV? Are you doing OK?"

"Yes. I've been fortunate and haven't gotten any bad infections. Moving here from the City has really helped. My T-cell count has gone up quite a bit." He appeared remarkably calm, almost happy, for someone facing a life-threatening situation. I couldn't accept it.

"What a heavy load to carry." I tried to offer him sympathy.

"It's not so bad." He deflected me. "Dialysis must be tough. How long have you been on it?"

I gave up trying to draw him out, and before Kurt and I took our leave, I briefly described what had happened to me.

On the way down the steep road from Mule Dung Ranch, my face streamed with tears and I told Kurt all that was running through my mind. How could Paul have compared my situation to his? How could he offer me sympathy when he was the one facing a life-threatening illness? Having no kidneys is nothing like HIV, I insisted.

"But without dialysis, you'd die," Kurt reminded me.

He had a point. I wiped away the tears and thought about Paul and AIDS. I wondered how old he must be, probably about my age, probably about thirty-four. That thought led me to remember Tom. He'd made it to thirty-four as I had, but then had died just four months after his birthday. I'd known Tom for nine years, but it wasn't until the very end that he told me the truth—that he had AIDS. Had he suspected that if I knew he was HIV-positive, I wouldn't have stood by and let him smoke and drink with such destructive intensity?

Unlike Tom, Paul didn't hide his condition, and he seemed at peace. He'd chosen to live each day as a blessing, a gift of one more day tacked on to what might be a very short life. I wanted to live like Paul, not like Tom. I didn't want to die. As Kurt turned the car north on Highway 128 toward Humboldt State Redwoods Park, I looked out across the rolling grass-covered hills that undulated golden in the California sun and counted my blessings.

Who Am I Now?

As the summer progressed, my lab values didn't improve. My phosphorus stayed too high and my creatinine, a byproduct of muscle activity, remained off-scale. Toni kept making adjustments to my dialysis to see if we could bring these values down. She was particularly concerned about the high creatinine, the main reason for my fatigue and nausea.

When she first saw my creatinine level at 15.1, she exclaimed that she'd never seen such high levels in a woman and only once in a male PD patient, a body builder! (A healthy person's creatinine runs between 0.5 and 1.2.) She hypothesized that several factors contributed to my elevated level. It seemed likely that my body was generating unusually high levels of creatinine because of my high muscle mass. She also theorized that my peritoneal membrane was highly impermeable. Creatinine is an unusually large protein molecule, and it appeared that I was having trouble pulling it through my peritoneal membrane during dialysis.

The bad news finally came from Dr. Goodman at the beginning of September. He told me that I had to stop walking so much, because even that small amount of physical activity was generating more creatinine than my body could handle.

Until Dr. Goodman ordered me to stop, I'd held on to a shred of hope that I could maintain some level of physical fitness. I could at least walk the Berkeley Hills on weeknights after dinner or the high trails of the Sierra on our weekend getaways. Dr. Goodman's order stripped away the last remnants of Lisa Before.

It was also at this time that I noticed how fast my body was aging. My skin grew dry and papery. No longer pale, it now darkened to an oddly deep, unnatural tan. The whites of my eyes turned yellowish and dim. My hair thinned, and though I'd always been blond, my body hair now developed a pale whiteness to it like that of an old person. Like an old woman, I'd also lost my period when I started dialysis. I sounded like an old phlegmatic smoker with my horrible hacking cough caused by the dialysate pushing stomach acid into my esophagus. I also ballooned up twenty pounds, a consequence of increasing my dialysate concentration, which resulted in my absorbing greater amounts of the dialysate's glucose. Strangest of all was the thick crusty whiteness that developed under the nails of my hands and feet. I couldn't scrape it away because it was connected somehow to the nails themselves. Dr. Goodman said it was a sign of poor dialysis.

I never once considered switching back to hemodialysis, despite the toll PD took on my body. Instead, I watched my body change with a kind of dispassionate objectivity, born of a paradoxical detente between paralyzing fear and grateful acceptance. I didn't want to die, yet it was obvious that the longer I remained on dialysis the shorter my lifespan would be. A transplant remained out of the question because my anti-GBM antibody levels were still too high. If I let it, the fear could easily spiral upwards and paralyze me in a coil of questions over which I had no control. Would Kurt no longer find me attractive, now that my body was deteriorating? Might he even leave me for someone else? What if I lost my job? What if I lost my health insurance? What if the anti-GBM disease never went away? What if I could never qualify for a transplant? What if I died?

Most of the time, however, the fear didn't gain the upper hand. Meditation helped reorient my perspective and let me see that I wasn't just my body. A consequence of this shift in consciousness was a pervasive sense of gratitude. PD kept me alive. I didn't feel great and I spent a lot of time tired, but I was alive. I could still enjoy sunny days, the beauty of nature, time with Kurt and my family. I was still here.

Without all the energy that had once kept my mind and body pulling me in a thousand different directions, I now found myself able to focus on the few things I could accomplish. I no longer pressured myself to be more than I could be. I relinquished grandiose aspirations and fantasies in favor of day-to-day functioning and surviving life on PD. With this relinquishment came a simplicity of consciousness that nourished a profound peace. There were moments when I actually felt happy.

Chapter 9 - Wait

Reaching Zero

When I was first diagnosed with anti-GBM disease in January, Dr. Pali said it could take anywhere from six months to two years for my antibody count to reach zero. The first antibody count was over four hundred. In February, it fell to two hundred and sixty two. I was tested every month, but the results took so long to arrive in the mail that sometimes they came just before I was due for my next blood draw. Each month felt like an interminable waiting game, checking the mailbox day after day to see if they'd come.

Every month I hoped the numbers would fall further, faster, but as the overall number decreased, so too did the rate at which it fell. I was surprised when Toni called me in early September to discuss my August labs, since my July antibody count had been twenty, still a long way from zero.

"Lisa, I've got great news!" She sounded excited, so I tore my gaze from the computer screen where I was working on the latest BoldVision pitch and focused on what she had to say.

"Your anti-GBM antibody count is now five. That's within normal range. It means we can put you on the schedule for a transplant."

It took me a second to disconnect my brain from work and switch over to talking about my health.

"Normal range? But shouldn't my antibody count be zero?"

"Normal range is zero to five, so you're good to go."

"I can't believe it!" I closed my eyes and thanked whatever higher power might be out there.

"I'll fax over the results so you can see for yourself. The transplant orientation will also help make it feel more real for you."

She told me the date of the orientation and I dutifully wrote it in my Franklin Planner. I hung up and rushed to the fax machine in the kitchen, grabbed the results and hurried back to the privacy of my office. I closed the door and stared at the piece of paper in my hand. There was very little on it, simply my identification information, the hospital letterhead, and my anti-GBM antibody count, but I read it over and over again, tears blurring my vision.

I wondered, had my daily meditation practice helped bring down the antibody count so quickly? Had it given me some power to eliminate the disease? I hoped this was true, but there was no proof. Though it had only taken eight months to reach "normal," much less than the two years I'd feared, the time seemed plenty long. Before this moment of holding the results in my hand, a transplant had felt impossibly remote. My entire focus had been on the present moment and the day-to-day survival on dialysis. Now, for the first time in a year, I let myself imagine the future.

Transplant Orientation

Within a week, I received a call from the transplant coordinator. She invited us to come to an orientation held every few months to educate patients due for kidney transplants. The orientation would take most of the day, so Kurt and I made arrangements to miss work.
On one of those beautiful September days when the summer fog finally lifts and the air radiates the warmth before winter, Kurt and I inched through the morning rush hour over the Bay Bridge, across the shimmering water, and into San Francisco. Kurt was skeptical about the timing of our trip.

"Don't you think this orientation is premature? You still have to wait another six months before the transplant."

"Maybe, but they went out of their way to invite us, and I think it's a good idea we get all the information we can, especially since you're going to be the donor."

The thought of Kurt's kidney being removed from his body and put into mine stopped us both short. Neither of us was ready to think about that, so we avoided the subject while we hurried to find parking and make it on time for the 10 a.m. meeting.

The transplant office occupied the fourth floor of a building across from the hospital's main campus in the well-to-do Pacific Heights section of San Francisco. A petite older woman in a white coat, navy skirt and matching low-heeled pumps met us in the hallway, clipboard under her arm and cheerful smile on her face.

"You must be Lisa and Kurt. Welcome! I'm the transplant coordinator. Right this way."

She led us to a conference room where three people sat around a large table waiting for the meeting to start. Kurt and I took seats on the far side.

"We're almost all here now. Let's see." The coordinator looked down at her clipboard. "Just one more and we'll be ready to start." Her pumps clicked briskly on the linoleum as she went out.

An uncomfortable silence filled the room while we waited for her to return. Kurt looked over the packet of information and the schedule of the day's activities. I pretended to do the same but surreptitiously studied the group, curious about the other people in our situation.

A couple sat across the table from us. The thin young woman looked healthy and like she was in her early twenties, whereas the young man seemed older, prematurely aged by poor health. It was obvious that he was the one who needed the transplant, his skin tinged yellowish from incomplete dialysis, or possibly jaundice, and his hair too thin. He looked as tired as I felt. They began whispering to each other in hushed voices, the young woman animated and smiling. I wondered about their relationship. Neither wore wedding rings, so they could be siblings, though she had dark brown hair and he was blond.

To the left sat a middle-aged, Asian man dressed in a designer sweat suit. He looked perfectly healthy as far as I could tell. Like Kurt, he was reading over the packet of information and sipping from a Styrofoam cup.

Just then, the coordinator hurried back in, accompanied by an overweight, middle-aged woman wearing a shapeless purple floral dress, much like the one I was wearing. She was apologizing profusely.

"I'm so sorry to hold you up. I had no idea the drive from Fresno would take so long, and the traffic across the Bridge was atrocious!" The woman rushed to squeeze into the seat next to mine.

"Hi," I greeted her and shifted my chair closer to Kurt to make room. I was surprised to hear she'd driven all the way from Fresno, but I soon learned that many people living in other regions of northern California traveled to San Francisco for specialized medical procedures like kidney transplants.

The transplant coordinator began the program. She spoke at length about the issues involved in a kidney transplant, her graphic slides keeping the talk concrete. My reaction to her presentation surprised me. I had entered the room confident and fairly relaxed, but now anxiety gripped me. When the photograph of a large, fleshy human kidney suddenly appeared on the screen, I was overwhelmed by a violent visceral response. The reality of what was coming hit me, physically as well as emotionally. My pulse pounded, my armpits drenched with sweat, and I grew nauseated. I gripped Kurt's knee under the table in an effort to keep from passing out.

"You OK?" He whispered in my ear. His hand was sweaty when he took mine, but he otherwise appeared calm. He squeezed my hand reassuringly.

While the coordinator moved on to the next slide, I relied on the relaxation techniques I'd learned from meditation. I closed my eyes and focused on breathing. As I struggled to regain composure, I realized how frightened I was by the idea of another surgery and how much I'd come to associate hospitals with horror. I'd avoided remembering the difficult hospitalizations of the previous winter and spring over the summer, as my life reached some kind of equilibrium.

The next slide distracted me from my hospital fears. It listed the average lifespan of the different kinds of kidney grafts: identical twin, living related, living unrelated, and cadaver. Because of the lag time involved in transplanting a cadaver kidney, which causes kidney trauma, its average lifespan was only ten years. A graft from an identical twin had the longest survival rate. Being genetically identical, the transplanted kidney had the same longevity as the donor's remaining kidney, and the identical twin didn't have to take kidney-impairing immunosuppressants. Living related and living unrelated donors had the same average lifespan: sixteen years.

"Only sixteen years? But that won't even put me at fifty!" I whispered to Kurt.

"Yeah, but who knows what medical advances will happen by then. You might even be able to clone your own kidney." He didn't sound worried.

I couldn't maintain his level of optimism. What if his kidney didn't survive? Hell, based on those numbers, would I be looking at dialysis again in sixteen years? I took a deep breath. Maybe Kurt was right. Maybe if I could hang onto the kidney long enough, technological advances would make it possible to clone one of my own kidneys, and then I wouldn't have to take immunosuppressants the rest of my life.

The coordinator opened the meeting to questions and I forgot my concerns when the young couple spoke. My assumptions had been off base. Though I was right that they were brother and sister, they had actually both suffered kidney failure. A rare inheritable genetic disorder had destroyed their kidneys. Jennifer had received one of their mother's kidneys a little over three years ago. Jeffrey had acquired one of their father's kidneys nine years previously, but it had stopped working and he was back on hemodialysis. He'd been on the national waiting list for a cadaver kidney for the past two years, and I guessed he was attending the orientation because they thought he might soon get a transplant. As far as I could tell, Jennifer had come along simply for moral support.

DIALYSIS: A MEMOIR

I felt contradictory emotions as I heard their story. On the one hand, my heart went out to them—so young to have gone through so much, a whole family impacted by kidney disease. But I also couldn't help feeling thankful about my own situation. My disease hadn't struck until my mid-thirties, and I'd had all of my twenties to revel in oblivious good health. I thought of my own autoimmune disease and hoped Kurt's kidney would be safer in me than Marla's or Mom's, my body less likely to attack an unrelated kidney, and I thought how lucky I was to share more antigens with him than with Marla or Mom.

The head transplant doctor made a guest appearance during the orientation. Dr. Brass gave a brief speech and further clarified the downside of dialysis.

"Dialysis keeps you alive, but it's hard on the body. You should be aware that for every year you're on dialysis, your body ages two years. A transplant is a much better option."

Listening to him speak, I remembered our last meeting in January and Mom's contentious interaction with him when we'd first discussed my transplant options. Though he'd changed his image, abandoning the brown corduroy for a more formal navy coat and red tie, his attitudes hadn't changed. He still strongly promoted kidney transplantation. After enduring nine months on dialysis, I now wholeheartedly agreed with him.

The orientation concluded with a presentation by the transplant team's social worker, who discussed the financial implications of a transplant.

"All of you here today are lucky enough to have private insurance, but if your situations were to change, you should understand how Medicare's restrictions might affect you in the future. Medicare covers the cost of kidney transplant surgery, a one time cost of about twenty five thousand dollars. The immunosuppressant medication costs less than ten thousand dollars a year, but Medicare only covers three years of the medication, despite the fact that you'll need to take the drugs for the rest of the life of your graft." Her expression darkened.

"Medicare does, however, cover dialysis completely, which costs upwards of fifty thousand dollars a year."

"How ridiculous!" I whispered to Kurt.

I couldn't believe the system was so ass-backwards. I now understood why there'd been so many poor and disabled people at the hemodialysis clinic. It was hard to believe the government could be so wasteful, yearly shelling out almost five times as much money for a person on dialysis than for a person with a transplant.

I remembered Maisie at the hemodialysis clinic, who'd felt so disempowered. It seemed like the government was forcing poor or disabled people to remain on hemodialysis, where the nurses could control their care, because the government didn't trust the patients to take care of themselves. I could imagine some Congressman saying, "We don't want to waste precious kidneys on people who aren't responsible enough to take their medications like they're supposed to." I again counted my blessings that I had insurance and that Kurt as well as Mom and Marla qualified as potential donors.

As we drove home from the orientation, the fog teasing the western edge of the City and the Golden Gate Bridge, I talked to Kurt about the future.

"Maybe it will all be OK after all." I looked out the window and allowed myself to entertain thoughts of the future. "Maybe we'll do the transplant and everything will be fine. Thank goodness we have excellent medical insurance!"

Kurt nodded. "February is a good time for the surgery, since the weather will probably be crappy. I won't miss too much biking."

The six-month wait was on.

Out of the Frying Pan...

One day in early October, I got a call from Cara.

"Hi there, Kidneyless Wonder, how's it going?"

DIALYSIS: A MEMOIR

"Long time no talk! When did you get back from your honeymoon?" I hadn't spoken with her since August, before her wedding.

"Can you talk right now? Good. Close your door!" Cara sounded excited and as dramatic as ever.

"OK." I closed my office door. "How was Morocco?"

"Wait, wait, wait. I'll tell you all about that when we get together. But hey," her voice dropped to a stage whisper. "How would you like to come work for me at ITWear? Things are crazy wonderful over here, I'm so busy and so much is going on. We just acquired two companies and our stock's really taking off. You should definitely buy some. But boy could I use your help! You wanna be ITWear's new PR Manager?"

"Wow, what an offer," I grinned, happy to hear her cheerful voice again. "It sounds great. But," I paused, remembering my health situation. "I don't know about the whole health insurance thing and my being on dialysis. I'll have to look into it."

"I'll talk to our HR gal here. I bet it won't be a problem switching carriers. Now, let's set a date to get together. How about doing dogs at Albany Shores on Saturday?"

We set a time to walk our dogs. I hung up the phone, my mind reeling with the pros and cons of her invitation. To go from Account Executive at a PR agency to PR Manager at a rapidly growing Internet software company would be quite a career leap. I also missed working with Cara. Though I'd established a polite, if awkward, working relationship with Rochelle, my experience at the agency had become just a job, where I simply went through the motions without any heart in it.

And yet, if I left this manageable routine, would I be able to handle working in a dynamic, demanding and stressful environment? Would I be able to keep up with the requirements of the new position, or would I become hopelessly exhausted?

After speaking with ITWear's HR person about their health insurance, I found the position even more attractive. It turned out that as long as I had no lapse in coverage my being on dialysis wouldn't qualify as a pre-existing condition. Thanks to President Clinton, if I paid my COBRA premiums for the month of December before the new health insurance kicked in, everything would be fine.

Just when I was about to accept Cara's offer, another factor entered the equation. My September labs revealed that my anti-GBM antibody count had climbed to six. Terrified the anti-GBM was returning, I immediately called the transplant coordinator. She told me to talk to Dr. Brass about the results and how they might affect the transplant timing. He was resolute.

"Research indicates that with anti-glomerular basement membrane disease the antibodies will burn themselves out over time and not return once they are completely gone. A count of six, however, is too high. We can't begin timing the six-month countdown until your values are safely within normal limits."

Oddly, Dr. Brass's declaration that anti-GBM once gone would stay gone I found comforting, though it contradicted Mom's research that indicated anti-GBM did return in a few rare cases. I wanted to believe him. But why had my antibodies gone up? Did contemplating the move to ITWear stress my body into generating more antibodies? Would moving companies cause even more stress and lead to an even greater increase in my antibodies? Mom suggested I use a logical method to determine my job choice by making a list of the pros and cons of working at both places. The result was obvious, and I prepared to tell Helen the news.

After the drama of Cara's departure from the agency, I worried how Helen would react to my news. I thought about simply telling her I was going to work for another company and not reveal I was going to work for Cara, but she'd guess the truth the moment I told her the company name. I decided to write her a memo before actually speaking to her, which would give me control over the communication and give her some time to process the news before responding. The memo said nothing of Cara and simply relayed the facts of my career opportunity at ITWear. My heart thumping, I emailed the letter before I left on Friday evening.

The next Monday, I approached our weekly staff meeting with trepidation. Would there be a scene? Would Helen order me out of the office as she had Cara? I joined the circle of co-workers, my palms sweating as Helen began the meeting. After covering a few routine agenda items, her next words astounded me. She didn't look at me when she spoke.

"Everybody, I'm sorry to say that Lisa is leaving us. Next Friday is her last day. We will have a good-bye party for her next Thursday." Her blue poker eyes met mine. "Make sure you offload your duties to Rochelle."

No mention of where I was headed and no reference to Cara. She glibly moved on to the next topic. Rochelle merely arched her brows in surprise at the news. I knew she'd corner me after the meeting, since my departure was going to leave her in the lurch until someone else could be ramped up to assist on the BoldVision account.

Relieved, I thought everything had been handled about my leaving—that was until the following Thursday. We all sat in the conference room with the good-bye party underway, when the agency's accountant approached me.

"Lisa, can I have a word with you?"

She led me to my office and proceeded to demolish much of the goodwill I'd felt for Helen. She informed me that I was responsible for paying back the work time I missed when going to the hemodialysis clinic. In order to not "incur any hardship" (her words), the agency would extract this money from my last paycheck and accrued vacation time.

What could I say? Helen and I had never officially discussed the agency's policy for my going to the clinic. I had, perhaps naively, perhaps arrogantly, assumed she thought I was worth it as an employee to be paid full time during those several months I was on hemodialysis. The end result was that I never did receive a final paycheck. Helen had achieved her revenge for my defection. I had few regrets when I left for my new job.

...And into the Fire

The next Monday I found myself thrown into the fantastic whirlwind of an Internet software company in 1999, moving full steam ahead following its IPO. My first day began smoothly enough. I reveled in the new drive to work, no longer chugging through the stop and go misery of commuters struggling to get to the Bay Bridge, a mere two freeway miles that took twenty long minutes. Instead, I cruised along scenic Wildcat Canyon road through Tilden Park and over the Berkeley hills. Despite being early winter, the day was sunny and the green eucalyptus and pine trees offset the brown-dead grass hills. I smiled, listening to NPR and enjoying the scenery, and congratulated myself on the improved commute, even if the tight curves required more attention.

ITWear was located in one of the small exclusive towns east of the Berkeley hills. The golf course and country club spread out on one side of the town, and the single main street displayed an understated elegance reminiscent of the pricey communities on the Peninsula across the Bay. When I arrived at one of the only stop signs in town, a local police car approached from the intersecting street. The officer studied my Toyota Corolla, notable among the BMWs, Mercedes and upscale SUVs around me, and then he briefly scanned my face. I made sure to come to a complete stop and count to three before I continued, conscious of my privilege as a white woman at the moment, despite my lack of kidneys.

I arrived at 8:30 a.m. and found the parking lot full. ITWearians began work earlier than my co-workers at the agency. I pulled out the handicap placard and took one of the three disabled people's parking places. I typically avoided using the placard, since I felt other, more disabled people should have the advantage of the special parking spots, but in this instance, it looked like there weren't any disabled people at

DIALYSIS: A MEMOIR

ITWear except me. I gathered together my purse, notebooks, and Franklin Planner, but I left the dialysis supplies in the car until I could check out the situation in the office.

As I walked around the side of the building and past many expensive cars, I noticed a jaunty silver Porsche illegally parked beside the front door, the vanity plate reading "ITWear 1." It had to be the CEO's car. I looked down at my shapeless blue dress, the sensible shoes, my protruding stomach, and tried to swallow the nervous rush of fear and inadequacy. Though I'd worked in high tech PR for more than two years, I'd led a sheltered existence in small agencies, the last with only seven employees, all women, and my first agency had only had four employees. Even then, I'd spent most of the time secluded in my office.

I struggled to push open the heavy glass doors emblazoned with ITWear's logo and found myself inside a company of almost three hundred people, moving fast, thinking faster, and talking a mile a minute. People rushed back and forth between the cubicles on the first floor, and more hurried up and down the exposed staircase to the second and third floors. Already feeling tired and weak, I didn't attempt the stairs but waited for the elevator with several older overweight women. I noticed one of them was the HR person who'd interviewed me.

"Hi, Lisa. Welcome to ITWear." She turned to the other women as we boarded the elevator. "This is Lisa. She's our new PR Manager."

They greeted me energetically, and their enthusiasm helped me overcome my sad memories of my prior life, when I used to spring easily up the five flights to the agency.

Cara had warned me that our desks were located in the executive suites where things could get pretty crazy, but I still wasn't prepared. I opened one of the dark oak double doors and entered pandemonium.

"Hey Cara, when's Jason Burrows going to call me?" A male voice shouted through the open door of the corner office.

I glanced through the glass and saw a man with Robert Redford good looks, in his late thirties or maybe early forties, staring intently at his computer screen, a telephone to his ear. A small TV sat on a shelf above him, tuned to CNBC, a talking head, stock tickers flying by on the screen, the volume blaring. The nametag on the door read, "Percy Johnson." ITWear's CEO and President waved a casual greeting over his shoulder when he spotted me.

"Any minute, Percy, I'll let you know." Cara called out over a low modular wall that subdivided the main room of the executive suites.

All the executive offices had glass walls and all their doors opened onto the main room, creating a fishbowl effect. I walked around the divider and found Cara seated at a desk by the window.

"Hey Lisa, welcome to ITWear. Here's your desk." She pushed aside a pile of folders and magazines to clear a space on the counter beside hers. "I'm sorry it's such a mess. As you can see, it's not exactly like the agency."

Just then the phone rang, and she swept into motion.

"Hi, Jason. How're you doing? I hope those martinis weren't too much for you last night." She bubbled with infectious laughter. "Sure, I'll get him for you." She muted the phone and yelled over the divider. "Hey Percy, Jason's on!"

I put my belongings down and turned on my computer. It asked for a password, which I didn't have.

"Oh, I forgot to get IT Help up here to configure your computer, I've been so busy. Sorry! Here's the IT guy's number. He's great." Cara's phone rang again and she launched into another animated phone conversation.

ITWear had just acquired two other companies and IT Help was swamped assisting the new employees, so I had to wait for the IT guy. In the meantime, I worked to impose order on the chaos, one of my specialties and a primary reason Cara had hired me. Our "desks"—more like two computers on a single counter—sat directly across from two other executive offices. The corner office on our side of the suite housed ITWear's CFO. I could see him through the glass wall, sitting hunched over a stack of paper, two older women seated beside him. From what I could hear of their conversation through the open door, they were discussing ITWear's quarterly numbers. There was some disagreement.

"I don't see how our net loss would equal this figure, not if we exclude the stock-based compensation expenses and integration charges." He jabbed the page on the desk with his left index finger. The two women sprang to their feet and bent over him to peer more closely at the earnings statement.

The double doors to the executive suites burst open and the biggest golden Labrador puppy I've ever seen lunged around the corner of the dividing wall and immediately thrust its panting, snuffling nose into my bag on the floor, obviously after my lunch.

"No!" I told the dog and pulled the bag off the floor and onto my lap.

"Sorry about that." A tall, boyish-looking man, wearing Khakis and a blue short-sleeved polo shirt that showcased his bulging biceps, appeared at the end of the dog's leash. "I'm Matt. You must be Lisa. This is Luther." With one hand he grasped the large black leather leash to reel the dog back, and with the other, he reached out to shake mine.

"Nice to meet you," I said, tucking my lunch safely on my desk behind a pile of magazines.

Matt yanked Luther into his office next to the CFO's and shut the door. By the time the IT guy showed up, Matt had left, either for lunch or a meeting, and closed his office door. Luther plastered his wet muzzle against the glass wall of Matt's office, furiously barking his loneliness and rage at being abandoned.

"What did you say my login was?" I raised my voice over the din when the IT guy didn't hear me the first time.

Meanwhile, Cara's voice blended with the CFO's, and Percy's periodic exclamations rose above everyone to yell, "We're up to thirty dollars a share!" Luther barked some more.

LISA FRIEDEN

By 2:30 p.m., I thankfully escaped the chaos and went outside to the relative quiet of the parking lot. I retrieved the bag of dialysate and walked around to the back of the building, where ITWear's lunchroom was. Various people were there, munching on free pizza and pouring Peet's coffee into their blue signature ITWear mugs. Though several people spoke to each other, I wasn't the only one who seemed not to know anyone. Self-conscious, I had to wait my turn for the microwave. I smiled when I made eye contact but didn't offer any explanation for the bag I put in the microwave to heat. With a sigh of relief, I hurried back outside to the privacy and quiet of the Toyota.

While I waited for the drain cycle to complete, I leaned the car seat back and closed my eyes. I'd brought along the earnings press release to edit, but I felt too tired to do much more than rest quietly and try to avoid worrying.

Had I bitten off more than I could chew? Would I be able to handle this job—especially since it felt like my whole day so far had been spent handling fire drills rather than completing any actual PR work? Cara had also just told me that she'd fired the incompetent PR agency, which meant I'd have to interview and hire a new agency, on top of everything else that needed to get done.

As I sat thinking, I noticed a man in one corner of the parking lot washing cars. After a while, I realized he was detailing them. When I finished my exchange and started back to the building, he was working on the Porsche with the ITWear vanity plate, despite the fact the car looked immaculate to me.

"Nice car." I smiled a greeting when I passed the man.

"Ain't she a beaut? Mr. Johnson has excellent taste in cars." He said this with pride as he wiped the sweat from his forehead with one forearm and went back to carefully buffing the CEO's car.

I couldn't remember when we last washed our Toyota, and we'd never had it detailed. Cars had never been something that either Kurt or I valued as anything beyond a means of transportation. I took a deep breath as I pushed open ITWear's heavy glass doors again. I had entered a whole other world taking this job.

Sex on the Job

Unlike the agency, no one at ITWear except Cara and the HR person knew of my health situation. I avoided using the handicap parking at the front of the building, except for that first day at the company. With the transplant not too far away, Cara and I hoped I'd be able to transition smoothly into a "normal lifestyle" after the operation. She suggested we not publicize my illness.

"People here don't know you like I do, and they might—you know—be a little weirded out."

I knew what she implied—that they might be prejudiced against someone who wasn't healthy like they were.

This thought left me feeling particularly self-conscious, especially since my new job entailed much more public exposure than the other PR jobs I'd held. I was expected to attend many of the marketing meetings, as well as converse with the sales department, not to mention with the executives and the general counsel.

My first Wednesday morning on the job, Cara breezed in.

"Hey Lisa-Lisa, we've got a noon marketing meeting. They're providing lunch! I think it's pizza. Oh, and I'll have to introduce you to everybody." Cara lowered her voice conspiratorially. "I'll also have to give you the skinny on Kristen and Tim, and Anna Joads, oh yeah, and on Tracy and Peter, too."

"That's a lot of skinny," I laughed, but grew apprehensive at the idea of meeting so many new people.

Cara grabbed me just before noon and led me downstairs, stopping to introduce me to various ITWearians.

"Isn't he a babe?" She whispered and looked back at one of the software engineers as he bounded up the stairs.

I followed her gaze and nodded, without actually finding the young man attractive. Sex was the furthest thing from my mind at the moment. I hurried to keep pace with Cara, feeling my swollen gut swing from side to side under my long denim shift. I clutched my lunch bag to my side.

Cara plunged into the crowded meeting room pulling me behind her and waving hello to people as we passed. She found us two seats at the far end of the table. Large boxes of pizza sat open on the table and a swarm of healthy, athletic-looking young people gathered about them, munching on slices and sipping sodas.

"That's Kristen over there," Cara whispered, her mouth at my ear. "She's our corporate communications manager. She's going out with Tim, our head of QA. Isn't she cute? They're such a great couple!" Cara rose and moved around the table to the people gathered by the meat pizzas.

I glanced down the table at the young woman, dressed in tight jeans and a tighter long sleeve yellow T-shirt. She looked happy and healthy, a big smile on her face between bites of vegetarian pizza. I opened my paper bag, removed the renal-friendly, unsalted chicken sandwich on homemade, salt-free bread, and took a bite. Memories of my awkward high school years sitting on the sidelines of the popular crowd overwhelmed me. Once again, I was the overweight, serious "geek-brain," the one who could never make pithy small talk or crack funny jokes, the one who sat on the outside looking in. The chicken tasted like sawdust.

Just then, Tony, our VP of marketing, rushed in.

"Hi guys, sorry I'm late." He took a seat at the head of the table. "Let's get started. I'd like to begin by introducing Lisa, our new PR Manager."

All heads swiveled toward me, greetings, curiosity and disinterest spread across the different faces. I smiled and waved at the group, trying to pass myself off as casually friendly. It worked, judging by the similarly casual smiles set my way.

DIALYSIS: A MEMOIR

During the meeting, I periodically tuned out and reflected on how different ITWear was from my last two jobs, which had been run by women. Before entering high tech PR, I'd taught Women's Studies, so it had been over five years since I'd been in a mixed gender environment, and over ten since I'd been in an integrated corporate setting. Maybe that's why I was surprised to find sexual politics alive and well. The men dominated the meeting, and when women interjected, they almost always began with an apology or some other kind of deferential statement to soften whatever point they were making. A few of the women seemed to secretly study each other, as if participating in some kind of covert beauty contest. No one looked at me.

As I walked to the elevator afterward, I realized I needed a new identity in order to navigate my way through this job. My weight, clothing, and lack of energy set me apart from most of the other people in the company, but few knew there was a medical reason. I pressed the elevator button and an overweight, older woman joined me for the elevator ride to the second floor.

"Hi, I'm Lisa, the new PR Manager." I introduced myself in an effort to be friendly.

"I'm Bernadette. I'm in finance. Nice to meet you."

When she stepped out of the elevator, I noticed the dress she was wearing. It suddenly occurred to me that the only other people I'd seen wear dresses at ITWear were the secretaries and the women in the finance department, all of whom were older, mostly married. With my long shapeless dress and bulging gut, I realized I fit in more with that crowd. To the rest of the marketing team, I must look like a frumpy old lady.

I adapted my behavior to suit my clothes, which wasn't difficult considering my reduced libido. While intrigue and gossip flourished around me, I moved about in a world of colorless asexuality. But it was a comfortable world, one that didn't threaten the status quo. In fact, as my time at the company lengthened, I found both security and freedom in the role I'd adopted.

Loving and Leaving

At home and in the privacy of my own mind, things weren't so clear. Kurt had fallen in love with a blonde Amazon, a cycling wonder with a hard body and boundless energy, but now my weight almost matched his, my body swollen, a twelve-inch tube protruding from my gut and taped across my non-existent waist. He still courted me for sex, and our sex life still continued, but in dark moments, I feared he'd run off with some young, healthy woman. I never voiced my fear nor expressed my wonder that he could still find me physically desirable. To say the words risked making my fears a reality. Instead, I disguised the fear behind a mask of confidence and acceptance of my situation.

Where I'd once been a jock, I now labored to create a new identity, one that radiated calm acceptance of my reduced circumstances. When Kurt approached me about a trip to Tahoe in December, my response was a masterpiece of studied nonchalance.

"Sure, go ahead. Have a great time."

Based on our experiences over the summer, I knew I couldn't stay overnight at Tahoe's high elevation without blood pressure problems. I would stay home. When Kurt expressed concern, I shrugged him off.

"Don't worry, I'll be fine on my own this weekend."

But as I spoke the words, a false smile pasted on my face, rage boiled inside me. I watched him happily pack his snowboard and gear, the picture of attractive, virile and vibrant health, and I was furious that he'd leave me to go off and enjoy himself doing something I couldn't do. And yet I felt it wouldn't be fair to demand he stay home. Besides, saying anything would reveal what I didn't want him to know: that beneath the calm, controlled image I projected, I was a seething cauldron of terror and need. If he knew any of this, he might really leave.

There was another reason for my silence. Our relationship, though intimate, had always been predicated on a high degree of civility. We respected each other's boundaries, striving not to violate them and risk infringing upon each other's psychological well-being. Heaven knows my emotions on any given day could run the gamut, so why dump something on him one day that would be gone the next? Both our family histories had been fraught with conflicts and drama, which probably contributed to our ongoing commitment to respect each other's emotional boundaries.

My fear, combined with this reticence, induced me to minimize the impact of my condition on Kurt. After he almost fainted on his first and only trip to the hemodialysis clinic, I never asked him to go back, and now, with me on PD and unable to share in the physical activities we'd once enjoyed together, I wouldn't ask him to stop them just to keep me company. Why should both of us suffer for what had befallen me? I wanted him as happy as possible. This, I reasoned, would increase the odds that he'd keep loving me and not leave.

Anniversaries

The days grew shorter and colder, the nights longer. My anti-GBM antibody count remained within normal limits, so it looked like the transplant was on for March. I watched the leaves change color and the seasons change with a profound sadness, remembering the previous year. Had it really been a whole year since my hospitalization? Had my kidneys actually died? Even now, a year later, it still seemed unimaginable that I had a twelve-inch tube surgically implanted in me and that when I sat on the toilet I couldn't pee. At the same time, the memories of "Lisa Before" were fading. She had been such a different creature than I was now.

I'd told myself a year ago that if I could just make it to Winter Solstice everything would be OK, but it hadn't worked out that way, the day passing instead in a blur of hospital procedures and my first dialysis. Now, I was determined to honor Solstice.

My parents, who'd come for the holidays, and Kurt's dad, who'd traveled from Chicago, had all enthusiastically agreed to a walk out on Nimitz Way in Tilden Park and watch sunset and the full moon rise. My dead legs struggled to keep up with everyone.

"We'd better hurry. The sun's almost setting!" Mom exclaimed, looking down across the Berkeley Hills to the Bay and San Francisco.

The winter sun shone low, distant and pale yellow in its southernmost arc over the City, the early evening remarkably calm.

"I can't believe it's so warm. It was five degrees when I left home this morning!" Kurt's dad chuckled. Kurt and I had sent him a plane ticket, since he belonged to the category of "starving artist."

"How're you doing, Lisa?" Marla called back.

"I'm hanging in there," I panted. Apropos words, I thought, as I climbed the steep hill to the lookout. I had hung in, I hadn't died. My legs plodded, my gut swayed, the heartburn surged, my heart pounded. I reached for Kurt's hand, and he helped me up the final climb.

"What a spectacular view!" Mom looked this time to the east.

The top of the hill offered a 360-degree panorama of the Bay Area and a clear view eastward, the San Pablo dam, the rolling grass and oak-studded hills of Briones Regional Park, the towns beyond, and the giant prominence of Mt. Diablo on the horizon. To the north across the hills, we could see the vast liquid stretch of the Sacramento Delta.

"Here, let me do the honors."

Bob took the white wine from Marla. She laid out the picnic on a blanket and we seated ourselves around the food.

Three young women sat near us, and as we ate, one began to play a drum. Another rose and began a provocative, sensual dance. A small stone arrangement, herbs, and a candle were laid out in front of them.

"They look like Wicca witches celebrating Solstice," I whispered.

"They could also be celebrating the full moon," Marla said.

As the sun sank into the City, more people rushed up the hill to catch the view and, by the time the sun finally set, more than twenty people had gathered to pay respects to Winter Solstice 1999.

"Here's to the end of the millennium!" Mom held up her glass.

Though I knew it meant instant heartburn, I took a token sip of wine.

I guess I can't party like it's 1999, I thought to myself.

Mom had her arm around Marla's shoulders. Kurt and his dad stood together talking quietly. Bob stood next to me.

Suddenly, whatever darkness I'd felt dissipated. A rush of thankfulness swept through me, to be here at this lookout with my family on the night of the last full moon of the millennium. I had made it another year, maybe not in full health and without my kidneys, but I was alive to enjoy the moment, grateful to be surrounded by my family in a place of beauty. It might not be perfect, but it was OK. It was what it was—no more, no less.

With the descent of the sun, a cool breeze picked up, presaging the emergence of the moon. On cue, the full moon emerged in the east, an enormous yolky presence, and the one woman's drumming grew louder, the other woman's dance more frenzied. A few other people began to gyrate and move in rhythm. As night descended, we took our leave, carefully picking our way down the steep hillside. I had to get home in time for the night's dialysis.

Crescendo

Over the next few months, I had little time to think about the upcoming transplant. The Internet bubble zoomed toward its hysterical zenith and ITWear's stock pushed past ninety dollars a share. Percy and the other executives seemed permanently drunk on the company's meteoric market capitalization and stellar national press coverage. Percy had become a Wall Street darling. Cara traveled with him to the East Coast on a press and financial analyst tour in late January, while I attempted to keep the PR situation on the home front under some semblance of control.

The high times culminated in a blowout bash ITWear threw one Friday night in early February. Initially, Kurt hadn't wanted to go, since he doesn't like crowds, but I wasn't going to take no for an answer.

"Let's go early," I said. "Before most of the people get there, and then we can leave before it gets really crowded. Besides, I'll have to get home in time to hook up, so we can't stay that long anyway."

We took BART to avoid rush hour and parking hassles. The Palace Hotel stood on Market Street directly behind the BART station. We walked the short distance and managed to dodge the spitting rain. Kurt pulled open one of the massive bronze-detailed glass doors and we entered the huge foyer, the ceiling rising over twenty feet, a kaleidoscope of crystal chandeliers winking and reflecting in the floor-to-ceiling mirrors that lined the hallway.

"Pretty fancy." Kurt looked around.

"I realize it's early, but where is everybody?"

We walked down the long hall past several locked doors until we saw a small sign reading "ITWear" clipped to a bronze pedestal.

"This must be it." I led the way into a cavernous room.

Tables laden with food lined the walls with workers in chefs whites standing at attention behind each of them. A few ITWearians sauntered between the tables.

"Is that a sushi bar? And that looks like a whole side of roast beast!" Kurt exclaimed, pointing.

Whatever concerns he'd had about the party immediately dissolved when presented with such a cornucopia of food. He moved purposefully toward the sushi chefs. I followed more slowly, taking in the decorations, the vast quantities of food, and the two mysterious fifteen-foot high figures on stilts that moved eerily about the room, wearing undulating, glowing neon wings.

"What do you make of that?" I pointed toward the female performer and her white painted face.

"Whoa!" Happy with his plate of sushi, he led the way and tried to elicit a response from the mime, but the woman didn't speak.

Instead, she began to juggle glowing balls. The growing audience cheered her on. We watched the performance and marveled at the spectacle unfolding in the massive, glittering room. In San Francisco, big space meant big money.

"This party must have cost a fortune. Do you know how much ITWear spent?" Kurt gestured at the endless tables and trays of food, the four different fully stocked bars, the winged performers.

"I have no idea."

As far as I could tell, no expense had been spared. We'd never been to such a party. ITWear's stock had reached ninety-nine dollars a share that day, and it seemed like the sky was the limit. Effusive excitement, intoxicated optimism, and hysterical enthusiasm radiated from the people entering the party.

As the ballroom filled with people, laughing, talking and drinking together, I began to feel self-conscious. I knew so few people at the company. I'd hoped Cara would show up early so Kurt and I could hang out with her and her husband; instead, I led Kurt uncertainly through the sea of unknown faces and took a place along one wall, where we unobtrusively watched the party swing into high gear.

An eighteen-piece band stepped on stage and began to play seventies disco covers at an ear-piercing volume. Eight sinuous, glamorous, and exotic dancers gyrated in front of the band and urged the crowd to dance. I longed to join the melee, remembering my wild college dancing days, but my body felt more like a lump of flesh than an electric spark on fire with vitality. I sipped my fizzy water and watched the fun.

The dancing reached a crescendo with the band's rendition of the Village People's "YMCA." Percy rushed onto the dance floor. The crowd parted for ITWear's CEO and several of the sales guys who followed him. They began lip syncing the song and boisterously angling their arms in the classic YMCA dance, the crowd laughing and clapping in drunken encouragement. As if that wasn't wild enough, Percy and the VP of sales began to leap frog each other across the floor. The image of tuxedo clad executives hopping about the floor made everyone break out into raucous cheers.

"That's our CEO," I yelled over the noise to Kurt.

"Our CEO would never ever do such a thing." Kurt's company had a much more conservative, perhaps more "traditional" CEO, though Internet companies hadn't been around long enough to develop such a thing as real tradition.

When the song ended, Percy appeared in front of us, wiping the sweat from his flushed face. I seized the moment.

"Hi Percy, I'd like you to meet my husband, Kurt."

"So you're the amazing young man I've been hearing about. What a love story—to donate your kidney to your wife! Talk about true love. Let me know if there's any way I can help. I wish you two all the best." Percy warmly shook Kurt's hand while Kurt and I struggled to keep the shock from our faces, then he rushed off through the crowd in search of another drink.

"You didn't tell me he knew!" Kurt exclaimed.

"But he wasn't supposed to! Only Cara and the HR person knew. Cara must have told him."

Cara and I had agreed to tell Percy before the surgery, but we hadn't yet discussed when. Cara had always been a sucker for love stories, so maybe she'd simply blurted it out. Whatever her motives, I trusted that she hadn't done it out of malice.

As I thought about it, I realized Percy had only mentioned the transplant and had said nothing about my current situation, which meant he probably didn't know what kidney failure entailed. Cara and I had planned that if everything kept on schedule, I'd have the transplant by March and then be able to blend seamlessly in with the other ITWearians. Percy loved making dramatic pronouncements, so if he now knew about the upcoming transplant, then who else had he told?

Denial or Delusion?

The answer came on the Monday after the party. In order to keep its incredible momentum going, ITWear planned to launch three new products, based in part on its acquisition of the two companies the previous fall. Marketing was in an absolute frenzy to get everything done in time.

Monday morning, Cara and I hurried to the weekly marketing meeting held in ITWear's biggest meeting room. I knew something was up when I took a seat next to Jenny, the manager of the Customer Care team. When she saw me, she put her hand on my arm to pull me closer.

"Lisa, I hope you don't mind, but I overheard Percy talking to Matt about you last week," she whispered in my ear. "I had no idea what you've been going through and that your husband is going to give you a kidney. What an incredible story!"

"Yes," was all I managed to say before Don, our Director of Marketing, began speaking.

"Listen up, everybody. We now have less than two months before we launch Distribution, Bulk Ticketing, and E-Education, and we still have a whole helluva lot of stuff to get done before then." Don hit a few keys on his laptop and the first slide of a PowerPoint presentation appeared on the screen at the far end of the room.

A bit later, his words caught my attention.

"March fourteenth is the deadline for Distribution. All the collateral has to be done by then. Where are we at with the Distribution customer brochure?"

While the tech writer responded, I realized that March 14th was just a month away. The product launches and the transplant were going to coincide. I looked down at the photocopy of the presentation and noticed the long list of action items that Cara and I had to meet as the publicity component of the three launches.

Just the week before, Cara had told me that I should take as much time off as I needed for the surgery and recovery, and that my health should come first. She'd said I shouldn't feel obligated to come back to work just because ITWear was attempting the unprecedented, simultaneous launch of three separate product lines.

But, as I looked at the long list of tasks, I knew I had to help in any way I could, especially since it was obvious there would be no way for Cara and the PR agency to meet the deadlines without my assistance. Even with my help, it looked dubious.

"Let's hear from the PR team," Don's words interrupted my thoughts. "Cara, what's the status of the Distribution press release?"

All eyes turned toward Cara and me. She sat next to me, looking healthy and beautiful. Her auburn hair, freshly dyed and washed, gently touched the crisp white of her low cut tailored shirt, her ubiquitous faux diamond earrings winking as she tossed her hair back.

"The release will be just fine, if we can get some decent customer quotes. We need good references, people who can talk about how they've used Distribution and liked it. The press couldn't care less if we're the only ones saying how great Distribution is."

DIALYSIS: A MEMOIR

A flush spread across her face as she looked fearlessly back at the Director of Marketing. Cara's job as PR person was to impose objectivity on Don's marketing mission and bring his grandiose visions down to size. This didn't make for a smooth working relationship.

I usually kept quiet during public meetings, preferring to speak privately with Cara and not draw attention to myself. Now, when I saw the frown crease Don's lips as he prepared to respond, I jumped in to defend Cara.

"Cara's right. We've got E-Team and NetLand on board as references, but we need a truly compelling customer reference for Distribution."

Everyone looked at me. Jenny wasn't the only one looking at me with curiosity. How many others had heard about my situation?

I dropped my gaze and studied the red and yellow flower bouquets on my long blue dress as I sought to overcome my self-consciousness and resume the calm, intelligent persona I'd crafted for myself at ITWear. I took a breath and looked up again.

"Let's face it," I said. "The two customers we have are little DotComs. Our story would be much stronger if we had a Fortune 500 customer who could talk. Don't we have any bigger customers we can talk to?"

"We have a lot of customers, don't we, Jenny?" Don said, ignoring the larger point I was trying to make.

"Let me see." Jenny rifled through a huge stack of paper in front of her.

Don didn't wait for her response. "No worries. I have it from Sales that we're signing several new contracts this week."

He further squelched Cara and my concerns by redirecting the meeting to a discussion of the ITWear website.

"I'm going to need your help figuring out how to get some publicity for Distribution if we don't have any big name customers," Cara whispered to me.

"OK," I nodded. I was already wondering how I could swing working from home as soon as possible after the transplant.

When the meeting adjourned, Jenny stopped me.

"Hey Lisa, I just wanted to say how much I admire you. I can't believe how well you're handling everything you've got going on." She shook her head. "I'm so impressed you're still working. If something like that happened to me, I don't know what I'd do."

"You do what you have to do." I shrugged, embarrassed.

I didn't want to be treated differently from other people, and I didn't want to feel like I was exploiting my situation for other people's sympathy, but it was too late. Like Percy, Jenny wasn't known for being reserved. As the days passed, more people approached me about the upcoming transplant, effusive with words of admiration and respect for how well I seemed to be handling such difficult circumstances.

Their concern underscored the truth that my life wasn't unbearable. Though I still had the nasty cough and heartburn and though I still had to hook up every night and once every afternoon, most of the time, I focused on my day-to-day activities without regrets or wishing that my life were different. Should I be more upset about everything that had happened to me? Was I in denial and hiding from my "true" feelings? Or, had my daily meditation and the Buddhist message of acceptance it reinforced deluded me from the "reality" of my situation?

I remembered Paul Monette, the AIDS novelist I'd written about in my dissertation, and his rebuttal to those who telescoped AIDS into a one-way ticket to death. For him, life was worth living and the story, the focus, should be on that life—not on impending doom.

As I reflected on Monette's message and my interaction with the people at ITWear, I had a revelation. We are all going to die—it's just a matter of when—but before then, our perspective is all we have. I could choose the perspective that I had fallen victim to a terrible disease and then experience the subsequent fallout of that way of thinking: the disempowerment, the pain, the suffering. Or, I could choose a different, more empowering perspective, and accept my circumstances, despite the fact that I had no choice about the initial disease that had changed my life.

And yet, though I felt uplifted by this revelation, deep fear still lingered. The anti-GBM disease might return, or some other, more horrible disease might leap out and attack. When these dark fears surfaced, I countered them with what I'd learned from Monette and from my meditation practice: now was what mattered. Those diseases were not here right now; therefore they were irrelevant.

Ironically, the more people talked to me about the upcoming transplant, the more I grew sick and tired of being on dialysis. When my time on dialysis was indefinite, I didn't resent all the hassles and hours needed for dialysis, but now I grew increasingly impatient for the transplant.

Dialing in Dialysis

With all the excitement at ITWear and my impatience for the upcoming transplant, I hadn't focused my attention on how PD was continuing to affect my body. I was surprised when I went to see Dr. Goodman for my check-up in mid-February.

"Look at that." He held my hands in front of me and pointed to the quick of my nails. "Do you see the pink that's beginning at the root of your nails?"

I held my right hand up and looked at my thumb. I noticed the thick crustiness under the nail and its yellowish hue. So much time had passed since these changes had disfigured my nails that I couldn't remember what they had looked like before kidney failure and I'd stopped paying attention to them. Now, I carefully examined the base of the nail. Sure enough, a little pinkish moon peeked out.

"What does it mean?" I looked up at Dr. Goodman.

He gave my other hand a squeeze and smiled. "It means you're being adequately dialyzed."

"Really?"

My gaze flew back to my hands and I stared at the fingernails and the growing pinkness. His words echoed in my head. After so many months and so many problems, my body was finally displaying a sign of improvement.

"I can't believe it." Tears flooded my eyes.

"The changes we're seeing probably reflect the adjustments Toni made to your dialysis back in September. I'm sure the fact you're no longer exercising is also helping to keep your body from overloading on creatinine."

Through the rest of our meeting and for days afterwards, I stared at my fingers. My body offered tangible, physical proof that it was making a slow steady return to some kind of health, much more compelling to me than the abstract numbers reported on my lab tests. I'd been so swept up in the holidays and events at work that I hadn't paid much attention to my body. Perhaps this unconsciousness was itself an indication that my dialysis was improving, since it's easier to be oblivious when things are working.

Now, each time I looked at my fingers and the growing pinkness, tears came, and I felt a heart-swelling hope. If for whatever reason the transplant didn't work, then maybe dialysis over the long haul might not be as bad as it had been for me at first. Perhaps if I had remained longer on PD, Dr. Goodman and Toni could have dialed it in to make me even healthier. Fortunately, however, I had a better alternative waiting for me. Within days of Dr. Goodman's observation, the transplant date was set.

Chapter 10 - Transplant

The Countdown

The transplant date was scheduled for the first week in March, but neither Kurt nor I had much time to anticipate the event. He was under deadline to finish debugging his company's software product before its release, and I was working frantically with Cara to nail down an East Coast press and analyst tour for the launch of the three new ITWear products. A phone message from the transplant coordinator brought it back to our attention one night, when we happened to arrive home from work at the same time.
"Kurt, you'll need to have your blood work done this week in preparation for the surgery on the 7th. You and Lisa will need to come in for your workup on Monday, March 6th."

Kurt's eyes met mine.

"I guess it's really going to happen," I said, circling the dates on the Ansel Adams calendar hanging on the wall.

Kurt took time out from work the next afternoon to have his blood drawn. We went about our business, not expecting any problems, but several days later, the coordinator left another message on the answering machine. This time, I listened to her message alone.

"Kurt, your lab values were fine, except your glucose was slightly high. As you know, we won't let anyone who is or who could become diabetic donate a kidney. But don't worry, lab values can fluctuate. So Kurt, can you come in and have another glucose test? Thanks."

I immediately called Kurt. My heart pounded and a sickening sense of foreboding shuddered through me. I needed his confident optimism to reassure me.

"Kurt, you won't believe it, but your glucose level was high. You have to have another set of labs done. But what if you can't donate? Your grandma was diabetic. What if you are?"

"Hold on a second, Lisa. What was high?"

"Your glucose levels. They won't let you donate if you're diabetic." Tears welled up.

"I know, I know. But who did you talk to? Who gave you this information?"

I told him.

"So what exactly did she say? Did she say I couldn't be a donor?"

"No. She said your levels were high and that you'll have to have another set of labs done to make sure it wasn't a lab error or random fluctuation."

"Fine, then that's what I'll do."

"But what if…?" I swiped at the tears, not reassured.

"There's nothing wrong with me. It was probably a lab error."

He sounded so calm and confident that for a second I cursed him, resenting and envying his rationality, which was, I sternly reminded myself, the reason I'd called him. I knew I was letting my fears blow the situation out of proportion, but even after hanging up the phone, I couldn't shake the sense of foreboding. The prospect of going under the knife again terrified me. Nothing before had gone like it was supposed to. Why should it now?

Breathe, I told myself. Be here right now, alive and standing in the dining room by the phone.

I went into the living room, pulled out a candle and the singing bowl, and sat down cross-legged on the zafu. Twenty minutes later, my watch timer beeped and I unfolded my legs. I struck the singing bowl and listened to its circling ring resonate into silence. I blew out the candle and got up. I didn't feel reassured, but I felt calm. An essence of acceptance whispered through me. I went into the bedroom and prepped the dialysis machine for my night session.

My fear that Kurt would be disqualified proved baseless. His second glucose test came back normal the next day. It turned out that coordinator had forgotten to tell him to fast the first time. Kurt had been right—he was fine. The transplant date remained set for Tuesday, March 7th.

A week before the operation, Kurt met the surgeon who would operate on Kurt. He came home with a glowing report.

"He seemed like a good guy, very matter of fact, and he knows what he's doing. He was one of the first surgeons to perform a laparoscopic nephrectomy, and since then, he's done over a hundred. He said the operation should take about four hours. He thinks I should recover in no time because I'm so fit."

"That's great," I smiled, relieved to see him enthusiastic about the upcoming ordeal. I wasn't sure what I'd have done if he'd felt as anxious as I did about undergoing another surgery.

Kurt had researched the different transplant surgical techniques, and when he learned about laparoscopic nephrectomy, he determined to have his kidney removed this way. Developed in 1996, the procedure enables the surgeon to obtain the kidney by going in through the donor's abdomen using a scope and specialized probes. Unlike traditional kidney extraction, which involves cutting through the muscle and sawing through one or more of the ribs in the donor's back (a painful procedure requiring a lengthy recovery), a laparoscopic nephrectomy causes the donor much less pain and enables a speedy recovery. The only scars come from the three puncture wounds where the scopes are inserted into the abdomen and a small bikini-line scar where the surgeon's hand enters the belly to remove the kidney.

"We're lucky the surgeon has moved out here," I said.

"I'm glad we didn't have to deal with the hassle of flying back to Maryland for the transplant. Who knows how long we would've been stuck back there."

Not to mention the insurance issues, I thought to myself.

As it was, ITWear's generous insurance package promised to cover most of the surgeries' expenses, Kurt's as well as mine. In the case of a kidney transplant, the recipient's insurance usually covers the donor-related costs. The fact that the doctor operating on Kurt was a true specialist and that the cost of everything would be covered made me feel more optimistic. These were good signs. Maybe everything would turn out all right, after all.

Work Up

On Monday, March 6th, we traveled to the transplant office for our pre-op work up. My parents came along, both for moral support and to make sure they were apprised of the particulars of each operation, especially since they would be taking us to and from the hospital when the time came. They had also been kind enough to agree to pet-sit Inu and feed MaxCat while we were in the hospital.

When we arrived at the transplant clinic, Kurt went to the social worker's office and the transplant coordinator handed me a lab slip.

"We're going to check your values one more time before the transplant. We also want to make sure your antigen status hasn't changed since your transfusion."

She directed us to the laboratory, which was on the first floor of the building across the street. Once we were outside, Bob headed off in search of Fillmore Street and a newspaper.

The laboratory waiting room swarmed with people, all talking.

"Oh geez," I muttered as we sat down. The other voices plus the television airing a peppy morning talk show drowned out my comment, but Mom still heard.

"What's wrong?"

"What if my antigen status has changed since the transfusion?" The fear welled up and overpowered my attempt to appear calm.

"It'll be OK. Even if you and Kurt don't share any antigens anymore, it doesn't mean they won't do the transplant or that the transplant won't work. You know that."

She used her reasonable, logical tone of voice, but I wasn't ready for logic.

DIALYSIS: A MEMOIR

"I do know that," I said. "It's just that it would mean we're not as compatible. What if—" I broke off, not wanting to utter the deep fear, but tears came, and the words followed. "What if, after all of this, I reject Kurt's kidney?"

"Don't think like that. The transplant doctors know what they're doing. If you have a rejection episode, they'll be able to handle it." She hugged me.

Her embrace reassured me and we rocked gently back and forth. For a moment, I was a little girl again being comforted by my mother, and then a voice at the front desk called me up for the lab draw.

Later, we all met up for lunch at a restaurant on Fillmore Street.

"I could've gotten out of it," Kurt said, sipping a fresh-squeezed lemonade.

"What do you mean?" I asked.

We all looked at him across the lunch table laden with dolmas, spanakopita, and other Mediterranean delicacies.

"You know the social worker was supposed to make sure I could handle donating a kidney, right?"

We nodded. They'd told us the purpose of the meeting had been for the social worker to conduct a final evaluation of Kurt's emotional suitability as a donor.

"Well," he continued, "She said if I wanted out, she'd make up a fictional medical reason to excuse me from donating. Just think, I could've gotten all those brownie points without having to lose my kidney!" The glint in his eye and tilt to his lips hinted that he was joking, but he also leaned over to reassure me with a kiss.

"What did you say when she asked you why you were willing to donate?" Mom drilled down, perhaps wanting to clarify Kurt's motives.

He drained his lemonade and looked smug. "I told her I wanted to donate for selfish reasons." He took my hands in his and his expression turned serious. "I want my partner back."

I smiled and gave his hands a squeeze.

His hope, and mine, was that with the transplant, I'd be able to regain my fitness and we could, once again, share the physical activities and outdoor adventures that had so strongly defined our relationship before kidney failure.

After lunch, we headed back to the transplant clinic to meet the surgeon who would put Kurt's kidney in me. As with Kurt's surgeon, we found him friendly and personable. He was a cyclist who commuted from San Rafael across the Golden Gate Bridge and into San Francisco.

"Your surgery will much easier than Kurt's," he explained. "And it'll take much less time. I expect no more than two hours. You'll be in the room next to his, and we'll coordinate the surgeries. We won't begin operating on you until we're ready to extract Kurt's kidney. We want to minimize the time his kidney spends unconnected to a blood supply."

For a moment, I thought of the fifty-thousand-plus people on the National Kidney Transplant Waiting list and their wait for a cadaver kidney. How lucky I was, how thankful, that Kurt could be my donor!

None of us was surprised when Dr. Brass kept us waiting upwards of an hour, but I was relieved that this time he and Mom didn't clash. Instead, he perfunctorily explained the major issues involved in the survival of the "graft," as he referred to Kurt's kidney. As before, he seemed completely optimistic. During the course of our meeting, he broke the news that I had forgotten I'd been waiting for all day.

"Lisa, your antigen status hasn't altered subsequent to the transfusion. You and Kurt still share two antigens, a fortuitous gift that gives the graft an excellent chance of long term survival."

We hit rush hour on the drive home because Dr. Brass had kept us waiting, but his words helped alleviate the pre-surgery jitters I'd been feeling and set the tone for the evening. Rather than go out for a fancy meal to celebrate my last "renal-friendly" dinner, we opted for a quiet night at home with Inu and MaxCat. I also had to hook up an hour early for my last night's dialysis if we were to make it to the hospital by 6 a.m. the next morning.

That night, as I went through the routine I'd learned so well over the past year, I thought little about what I was doing at the present moment. My entire focus was on tomorrow's surgery. Instead of fear, I felt a rush of excited anticipation. After so many months of waiting, the time was almost at hand. I adjusted the catheter beside me as I lay down and smiled to think that the next time I slept in this bed I would be free of equipment.

Bring It On!

Tuesday morning, March 7th, our alarm clock woke us at 5:15 a.m. I asked Kurt how he was feeling as we got dressed. He shrugged and began lathering his face for a last shave.

"As ready as I'll ever be. I'll be glad when today is over."

"Me, too," I said. "I am so ready for this surgery. Let's bring it on!"

"Yeah, bring it on!"

Our impatience didn't speed the surgery, however. We arrived at the pre-op waiting room at 6 a.m. as instructed, but then had to wait. My parents had driven us, and I had lugged along the dialysis machine, which Toni had requested for a new PD patient of hers. The cycler was in such high demand that she was going to come by the waiting room and pick it up.

Shortly after 6 a.m., Marla joined us, only slightly bleary-eyed at the early hour, and carrying a cup of Starbucks coffee. When Bob saw it, he hurried off to get himself a cup. Kurt picked up a newsmagazine lying on one of the tables. The rest of us sat about waiting, tired yet wired, restlessly making small talk and joking nervously. During the wait, Bob took a few photographs of us. Mom obsessed over the upcoming surgery. She kept imagining worst-case scenarios.

"What if you and Kurt are on the operating tables and then the Hayward fault goes? Or the San Andreas? It would be an utter disaster."

"Mom, just shut up!" Marla was appalled.

I understood the reasoning behind Mom's morbid speculations—after all, why not imagine the absolute worst-case? I'm pretty sure it gave her a feeling of control over the situation, because if anything less than absolute disaster happened, she could feel pleasantly relieved.

Kurt's wait ended when a nurse came for him at 8 a.m. His surgery would be much more involved and time-consuming than mine, since extracting the kidney was the most difficult part of the transplant process. In order to gain access, the surgeon would need to reach in through Kurt's abdomen, close off any open blood vessels, and carefully move aside other organs in order to remove his left kidney and ureter.

This part of the surgery would take about three hours, and then it would only take another hour or so to close him up. They wouldn't need me until about the three-hour mark, since they simply had to cut open my abdomen, attach the kidney to the left artery in my leg and the ureter to my bladder, and sew me up. My wait continued.

At 10:30 a.m., the nurse finally came. Marla accompanied me to one of the pre-op rooms. We were glad Mom stayed behind. I now felt quite apprehensive and didn't need gallows humor adding to the tension. The nurse told me to drain myself dry. I forgot they would need my peritoneal cavity empty for the operation.

"Ugh!" I groaned to Marla. "My gut's killing me. I'm not used to going dry."

I felt like a big bag suddenly squished flat, the peculiar, uncomfortable sensation of my abdomen folding back in on itself. I hoped I wouldn't have to wait much longer. Marla made small talk to distract me, but I had trouble concentrating.

The pain in my gut and the fear I felt for Kurt blocked her out. He was more than two hours into his operation. I wondered how it was going and hoped there wouldn't be any glitches. When the orderly finally came to wheel me to the anesthesiologist's room, I refused to lie flat on the gurney. The pain was too much. Instead, I sat hunched over my empty gut, anxious for the whole thing to get underway. The last thing I remember was an older man, his eyes behind steel-rimmed glasses matching the green color of his scrubs, smiling down at me and saying, "You won't feel a thing."

ICU

The next thing I remember was chaos. Beeping machines surrounded me: glowing monitors, numerical printouts, green graphic displays. Tubes stuck up my nostrils tickled me with the cool, dry flow of oxygen. A strangely diffuse pain pushed down hard on my gut, as if an enormous elephant sat on me. When I opened my eyes wider, I heard someone say, "She's awake!"

I looked up and saw Mom and a nurse standing by the bed.

"What time is it?" I asked.

"2:30 in the afternoon." Mom said.

"Really?" I was shocked. The surgery was supposed to have taken two hours, not more than three.

Mom explained that before I was transferred to the intensive care unit I'd had to wait in the post-op recovery room for the general anesthesia to wear off.

"Is that where I am now?"

"This is the ICU. Can't you tell by all those wires hooked up to you?"

Mom sounded calm, but her mouth looked tight, her face anxious and a little afraid, as she helplessly watched the nurse check several of the monitors and record some information in my chart. The urge to drift back to sleep seized me, but I fought it and followed Mom's gaze to the machines on the other side of the bed.

It was only then that I noticed the machines were beeping in response to my bodily functions. As if on cue, a blood pressure cuff attached to my right arm automatically inflated and then ticked down. Wires ran from my chest and abdomen to what looked like an EKG, and another device connected a wire from my left forefinger to a machine that monitored what appeared to be my oxygen-blood saturation. An IV pole stood directly above me and dripped several different lines into the vein on the back of my left hand. My last thought before drifting off again was that my time in ICU was going to be loud.

The next twenty-four hours were excruciating. The nurse had explained that if the pain grew too strong, I could push a button by the bed and receive a bolus of morphine directly into my bloodstream. Within hours, it wasn't the beeping of the machines or the pressure cuff on my arm or the nurses repeatedly coming into the room or the tickly dry air piped into my nostrils that tortured me, but the worst case of itching I've ever experienced. My skin felt like a million little bug feet crawled over it. Any attempt to scratch was foiled by the IV needle in the back of my one hand and the blood pressure cuff on my other arm, not to mention the web of wires running across my body.

It wasn't until late that night that I was lucid enough to realize I was having an allergic reaction to the morphine. Fortunately, once I told the nurses, they were able to switch me to Demerol without incident and, by the time I was transferred out of ICU and into a regular hospital room the next day, the itching stopped and I was finally able to sleep without severe discomfort.

Those first twenty-four hours after the transplant were critical because that was when there was the strongest possibility my body might reject Kurt's kidney. As a precaution, the doctors had dosed me with enormous amounts of the immunosuppressant medications Neoral, Cellcept and prednisone, which severely taxed my immunity—another reason they kept me in ICU. Fortunately, Kurt's kidney seemed happy in its new home, so except for the morphine misery, everything worked like clockwork for me. Unlike my traumatic experiences at the hospital in Berkeley, once I left ICU, my stay in San Francisco was wonderful.

DIALYSIS: A MEMOIR

The Cruise

Hospital policy placed spouses in separate recovery rooms to ensure that if one spouse had difficulties the other wouldn't worry. In our case, however, the staff relaxed its policy when faced with Kurt's insistence and Mom's indomitable will. This change to protocol was made even easier because Kurt's roommate had just checked out, leaving the other bed in his room available. By mid-Wednesday afternoon, Mom and Bob wheeled me down the hall to join Kurt.

"Wow, what a room!" I drank in the sight and scent of an astounding number of bouquets and plant arrangements. A huge number of white and silver balloons festooned the ceiling between the two beds. Kurt lay propped up on pillows, dwarfed by the large hospital bed. He looked scrawny in the pale blue hospital gown, tired, and a little yellowish, but he smiled at me.

"Welcome to the cruise ship!" He gestured around the room with a sweep of his arm.

Our experience in recovery did indeed feel like being on some kind of surreal cruise. Located on the fifth floor of the hospital with a west-facing window, our room had an ocean view that let us watch sunsets over the Pacific. Fresh flowers surrounded us, and our meals, as well as any snacks we might want, were served to us in bed. I no longer had to eat renal-friendly food, and the standard hospital fare wasn't too bad. We each had our own recliner bed, our own TV, our own remote control, our own nurse's call button, and we each had our own narcotic drip.

For our friends who couldn't come to the hospital, we had a web site, which a friend kept updated with information passed along by Marla. One of Kurt's fellow co-workers also sent daily emails to everyone at Kurt's company. We held court from our beds for those who did visit. Between the Harry Potter books a friend had lent us, visits from friends, cable TV, and a frequent dosing of narcotics, my recovery passed in an agreeable haze.

Thursday morning after breakfast, a large group of people in white lab coats pushed into the room, led by one of the transplant clinic nephrologists.

"Good morning. You both are looking well," the doctor greeted us with a congenial smile.

My bed was closer to the door, and I noticed that several of the group stood whispering to each other and looking at our flow sheets that were taped to the door.

"As I'm sure you are aware," the doctor continued addressing us, "we're a teaching hospital. Our fellows accompany us on our rounds."

The group of young people nodded to us. I don't know about Kurt, but I felt odd sitting in bed and being observed by so many people who weren't just looking back at me but studying me like I was some kind of specimen. I put on a cheery smile and took another sip of the warm prune juice, an aid for stimulating one of the prerequisites for leaving the hospital. The doctor examined each of our scars while several younger people eagerly watched, and then he looked at our flow sheets. He spoke to the group in a subdued voice but behaved for the most part like Kurt and I weren't in the room.

"You'll notice that their creatinine levels are mirroring each other. Quite remarkable." His finger traced the creatinine values that had been recorded every six hours on the flow sheets.

Murmurs and nods of agreement.

"And you'll notice the large urine output of the graft. Over eleven liters in twenty-four hours. Quite impressive!"

I looked over the edge of the hospital bed and saw that even now the yellow fluid was flowing down the tube and into the bag on the floor. I smiled, proud to see how well Kurt's kidney was dialyzing me.

During our operations, the doctors had inserted foley catheters into both our bladders. With his foley, Kurt didn't have to deal with the painful hassle of getting himself to the bathroom. In my case, they wanted to track the exact volume of urine produced by my new kidney. They also wanted to prevent any pressure buildup in my bladder, which could threaten the stitched junction where Kurt's ureter had been surgically attached to my bladder. With the foley in, I had no sensation of either the need or the act of urinating. I'd have to wait until checkout time from the hospital for my first "normal" pee.

Not All Smooth Sailing

My recovery proceeded exceptionally well, but Kurt wasn't so lucky. The doctors had told us to get up as soon as possible after the surgery and walk around. I had no trouble pressing a pillow to my gut and walking about the hospital halls, but Kurt suffered severe pain when he took anything more than a shallow breath. My efforts to cajole him out of bed didn't work past the first few times.

It was hard to sit still and keep him company, I felt so good. He stayed in bed while I walked around the fifth floor and discovered a spectacular view of the Golden Gate Bridge and Marin headlands from the northwest corner of the building, which became my destination for the several walks I took each day. The nurses didn't take Kurt's complaints seriously at first, because he downplayed his discomfort. By Thursday afternoon, however, he stopped acting stoic and was taken for a chest X-ray. Late that afternoon, his surgeon came to talk to us. He stood by Kurt's bed, so I sat up to listen.

"The X-ray shows that one of your lungs has partially collapsed," he said. "I'm pretty sure that's what's causing your pain. I think that when we injected the gas into your abdomen to perform the laparoscopic nephrectomy the pressure partly crushed the lung. But don't worry," he added when he saw Kurt's alarmed expression. "We have a technique that can easily fix the problem. I'll have the nurse up here first thing tomorrow morning. In the meantime, let's take a look at your scar."

Kurt pushed down the blankets and moved aside the hospital gown.

"I've got this big lump." He gestured to an area directly below the bandages and above his groin, which I'd seen earlier was an oblong, yellowish, almost tennis ball-sized lump.

"Ah yes, I see," the surgeon nodded. "That's a good-sized hematoma. How unfortunate. Apparently, I didn't sufficiently close off one of the blood vessels and you had some seepage."

"Is it still leaking?" Kurt demanded, again alarmed.

"I don't think so. It may look bad, but it's not that big a deal. What you've got is equivalent to a large bruise. Your body will absorb the old blood and break down the hematoma. Do you see how areas of it are already beginning to turn blue and purple?"

"How do you know I'm not still bleeding?" Kurt peered down at his groin, not reassured.

"I can't be one hundred percent sure, of course, but it's unlikely. Keep an eye on it and if it grows larger or if more yellow sections appear, let me know. But don't worry, I'm sure you're fine."

The surgeon's words did little to allay Kurt's concern, and every time he rose from bed for the next few days, he'd bend down to check the hematoma's size and coloring. Maybe it was the prednisone, or maybe it was because I physically felt so good, but unlike Kurt, I believed the surgeon and wasn't worried. My one sadness was that Kurt couldn't yet share with me the wonder of how good his kidney made me feel.

Friday morning two nurses wheeled in a large machine with tubes coming from it.

"It looks like a giant bong!" Kurt laughed.

One nurse frowned, but the other smiled as they quickly and efficiently hooked Kurt up, attaching a tube and mask to his face.

"OK, Kurt. I'm sure you know what to do," the smiling nurse said. "Breathe in now, as hard as you can."

She pushed a button on the machine. A motor kicked on, mist flowed through the tube, and Kurt inhaled deeply. Suddenly, there was a loud pop.

"Ow!" He let out a big groan and doubled over.

"How's that?" The other nurse helped him sit up and handed him his plastic spirometer.

(We'd been given these devices and encouraged to practice inhaling into them to build back our lung capacity following our surgeries. Kurt hadn't had much luck with his.)

"Let's see how high you can get it to now," the nurse said.

Kurt inhaled into his spirometer and let out a cheer. "Yay! I feel so much better."

The rest of Friday, Kurt happily strolled the hospital halls with me, only once stopping to check the size and color of his hematoma. I guided him to the spectacular viewpoint on the northwest side of the building. As we gazed across the brilliantly illuminated Golden Gate Bridge, I felt happy and complete, now that he was feeling better and could join me in celebrating.

"This place certainly beats the other hospital, doesn't it?" I said.

"It's good to be here, together." Kurt kissed me, and then, before the pain from standing grew too strong, we made our way back to our hospital room.

Preparations for Departure

Late Friday afternoon, a woman came into the room lugging a large cardboard box. She plunked it down at the foot of my bed and let out a sigh of relief.

"You're looking good. You must be excited to go home tomorrow."

I managed to catch the name on her tag and remembered her as the social worker who'd given the talk at the transplant orientation.

"I'm doing pretty well. And Kurt's doing well, now, too." I gestured toward Kurt, who looked up momentarily from Harry Potter and the Prisoner of Azkaban.

"I've brought you your first month's supply of medications, and we need to review the Kidney Transplant Manual."

I'd already looked over the post-op manual that the transplant nurse had given me the day before, but the social worker insisted on reviewing all forty pages in exhaustive detail. She rolled over my objections and, for the next two hours, I listened to her talk. First came the issue of the medications.

"The first six months after your transplant are the riskiest for rejection, so we start you on very high levels of the immunosuppressants. You'll take Neoral, a form of cyclosporine, Cellcept and prednisone. Your dosage of Cellcept won't change, but we may adjust your cyclosporine depending on the results of the lab tests you'll be getting on a regular basis. As you can see from the prednisone calendar," she handed me a sheet of paper, "you're now at sixty milligrams, but by the end of the first week out of the hospital, we'll bring you down to thirty. By the end of two months, you'll be down to ten milligrams. You'll need to review the calendar each week to make sure you're taking the correct dosage."

I nodded, studiously looking over the calendar and thinking how easy it was going to be to simply pop pills rather than go through all the intricacies and time commitment of dialysis.

"Unfortunately, a consequence of having depressed immunity is that you'll be at risk for several common opportunistic infections. We'll need to give you prophylactics to prevent them. The Mycelex troches are an anti-fungal drug to combat thrush."

She handed me a bottle, which I opened as she continued speaking.

"For the first three months, you'll need to suck on a troche after each meal. If you do end up noticing any white patches on your tongue or in your mouth, let the transplant nurse know. You'll also need to take Cytovene. It's an antiviral that helps prevent cytomegalovirus. You're also at an increased risk of pneumonia during the first three months, so you'll need the antibiotic Bactrim as a prophylactic."

I was taking all these medications while in the hospital, but the nurses simply handed me cups of drugs to take at various times of the day. Now I'd be responsible for the dosing and timing and, looking at the box of meds she'd brought, I realized exactly how much medication I'd have to take every day.

Her use of the phrase "opportunistic infections" made me think of Tom, of Paul Monette, and of the other people I'd known with AIDS, and it made me think of all the strange things that are out there, waiting to attack once the immune system is suppressed. Would I be faced with more health problems? The threat of future sickness cast a momentary shadow over my feeling of well-being. I now had an inkling of why some people didn't comply with their immunosuppressant drug regimen. The social worker kept talking.

"Drug compliance is mandatory. You must take all your medications exactly as prescribed. This means taking the exact dosages at the exact time each day you're supposed to take them. The long-term health of your kidney depends upon it."

"Of course," I nodded and took the bottle of prednisone she handed me.

"You'll save a lot of money if you use mail order to buy your medication, because you won't have to shell out co-pays for each month's supply of drugs. You'll be able to purchase a three month supply for the price of a single co-pay. The savings really add up."

I made a mental note to sign up for this service as soon as I got home.

"Now, let's talk about what to do in the event of a rejection episode," she changed the topic and pointed to the corresponding page of the manual.

"The most important symptom of a rejection episode is a fever of a hundred and one or higher. If you develop one, you'll need to immediately contact the on-call transplant doctor, so we can determine if it's truly a rejection episode and take the appropriate measures. There are several other symptoms to be aware of, these include: if you develop flu-like symptoms, or fluid retention, or pain and tenderness around the kidney, or if your creatinine begins to rise. If any of these things happen, you should let the transplant nurse know right away."

A rejection episode was one of my greatest fears, but before I had a chance to think more about that, she concluded her speech.

"Take it easy once you go home. I'll bet you're eager to go back to work, but make sure and allow enough time for your recovery. Once you return to your job, make sure to still get plenty of rest." She stood up and moved toward the door. "Remember, your immune system is now compromised. Stress can further deplete it and may leave you at a greater risk for getting sick."

I let out a big sigh, relieved when she left. If stress was bad for me, her speech certainly hadn't helped. I forced myself to focus on the last dinner of our hospital stay—baked chicken and pasta, with a peanut butter cookie for dessert. That night, I gave myself one final bolus of Demerol, determined to enjoy the last night in the hospital fully relaxed.

Saturday morning, Kurt and I awoke excited. The morning nurse arrived at 6:30 a.m. to remove our foley catheters. She came to me first.

"It may feel strange as I pull it out, and once I do, you'll probably need to go to the bathroom right away, so be prepared."

My mind spun with the realization that I was about to pee.

"I haven't peed in over a year," I said as she began to pull.
"Really? Well, here goes."

I gritted my teeth with discomfort as she removed the catheter. Immediately, I felt the need to urinate.

"You're right. I've gotta go!"

The nurse laughed and moved out of the way as I pulled a pillow against my gut, yanked the IV pole after me, rushed into our hospital room's little bathroom, and closed the door.

I threw my hospital robe on the sink and hurried naked to the toilet, though I still kept the pillow pressed to my bandaged gut. I didn't want any unnecessary impediments in the way of my first pee.

The toilet seat felt cool and I relaxed onto it. And then, just as I'd done for thirty-three of the thirty-four years of my life, I peed. As the warm yellow stream left my body, so easily and effectively emptying my body of toxins, tears filled my eyes. Before I knew it, I was crying hard.

There had been so many times over the past year that I'd sat on the toilet and tried to pee, futilely hoping that if I could imagine the pee flowing freely from my body my power of imagination would somehow bring back the ability. How strange it had been to sit and not pee. Now, everything seemed natural, normal again. A knock sounded on the door, and I grabbed some toilet paper to blow my nose and wipe my eyes.

"Are you all right?" Kurt's voice called through the door.

I opened it and moved into his embrace, ignoring the discomfort in my gut and the pillow between us.

"I peed," I said, and began to cry again. Kurt's body began to shake. I realized he was crying, too. In the ten years I'd known him, I'd only seen him cry twice before.

"Your kidney is working like magic." I pulled apart enough to look into his warm, wet eyes. "Thank you, thank you."

I kissed the tears on the side of his cheek and then moved to his mouth, my heart in the kiss. No words can convey the love I felt for him at that moment. I quite simply owed him my life. After several moments, I felt him smile against my lips.

"I think I've got to pee, too." He moved out of the embrace.

I wheeled my IV pole back into the hospital room, the pillow clenched to my abdomen, and eased myself back into bed. Reclining relieved the pressure gravity exerted on my gut when I stood, and it also alleviated some of the dull ache that throbbed from the seven-and-a-half-inch stitched incision curving from the left side of my waist down to the center of my groin. Just then, the nephrologist walked in.

"How're you doing this morning, Lisa? Ready to go home?"

"I just peed for the first time in over a year! I feel great."

While he looked at our flow sheets on the door and made some notes on a clipboard he carried, I realized that I spoke the truth. I felt good, really good. I wasn't tired, and I wasn't nauseous. In fact, I was desperately hungry for breakfast, which hadn't yet come. And, I needed to pee. I pushed myself out of bed.

"Excuse me, but I need to pee again!"

The doctor smiled. "It may take some time to build up the ability to hold much urine. Your bladder is kind of like a muscle, and when it isn't used for a long time, it shrinks and loses its tone."

I hurried past him and knocked on the bathroom door.

"Hey Kurt, I need to pee again. Bad!" My need had grown urgent.

"Just a minute."

"Hurry!"

Kurt came out of the bathroom, and I rushed past him. When I sat on the toilet seat and peed, I broke into tears again. Neither the novelty nor the significance had worn off. It still hasn't.

When I came out of the bathroom, the doctor was gone. Kurt gave me a big smile as I eased back into bed.

"The doctor says we're free to go. I can't wait to get out of here. Patrick just called and said he's coming up to spend the weekend with us."

"Excellent," I said. Patrick was our millionaire Silicon Valley friend and the reason we'd originally moved to the Bay Area.

"He's offered to be our 'boy toy' for the weekend and do whatever we need. I want to go on a hike this afternoon in Tilden. Patrick agreed to drive, since the doctor says we can't drive for the next couple of weeks. You want to come?"

"Are you kidding?!" I was incredulous. "We're just getting out of the hospital today. How about you wait and see if you feel up to it once we get home?"

Kurt frowned, but before we could discuss it further, my parents arrived. They had brought the Vanagon to take all the flowers and our other belongings back to Berkeley.

Several weeks of cold rainy weather had evaporated. Just five days after the transplant surgery, Kurt and I stepped out into a gorgeously sunny spring morning. I took the warm weather as a sign of hope. I pressed the pillow hard to my gut and clenched my teeth when the Vanagon lurched over the bumpy, uneven streets of San Francisco. By the time we arrived home, the desperate need to pee reminded me unequivocally that I no longer needed an artificial machine to achieve dialysis. Kurt's kidney worked wonders.

Chapter 11 - Back to Life

A Speedy Recovery

The most remarkable thing about the transplant surgery was how quickly we got back to our lives. When we arrived home late Saturday morning, Mom and Bob helped us find places in our small house for all the flowers. Then, as soon as Patrick joined us for lunch, Kurt broached the subject of a hike.

"So, besides Patrick and me, does anyone else want to go for a hike in Tilden?"

Mom was as incredulous as I'd been. "But you just got out of the hospital! And in case you've forgotten, you couldn't even get out of bed without trouble breathing until yesterday. You and Lisa should take it easy for a few days."

"Yeah, yeah." Kurt shrugged off her concern and resorted to his usual strategy for dealing with his mother-in-law: avoidance. "Does anyone else want to go?"

"I'll come," Bob said. "Would you mind stopping by our house? We can pick up Inu and Satie."

Inu was with Satie, the dog they were pet-sitting, at their house they were renting while Mom was on sabbatical at UC Berkeley.

"Sure." Kurt looked over to where I lay on the recliner couch, my lunch sitting on the pillow over my gut. "You want to come?"

"No thanks. I'm definitely not ready to go on any hikes yet. I'll make some calls and let people know we're out of the hospital."

After two small hikes in Tilden and a weekend of lounging around watching movies on our recliner couch, Kurt was thoroughly bored. By Monday morning, he had his laptop out and began tackling the enormous amount of email that had built up over the last week. He continued his speedy recovery and went to work in person the following Monday, just under two weeks since his surgery.

DIALYSIS: A MEMOIR

The Lab

The first week out of the hospital, I still felt a lot of pain when I sat upright or stood for any length of time, but as per transplant protocol, I had to go first thing Tuesday morning to have my labs drawn. Bob was kind enough to drive me to the local lab. According to the lab's answering machine, it was supposed to open at 8 a.m. I was shocked when we arrived early, at 7:55 a.m., and found a line of eight people waiting outside the locked doors.

"What's this?" I exclaimed, unfastening my seat belt.

Bob locked the Vanagon and followed me over to the line, which consisted of a mix of elderly men and several working-age men and women dressed in office clothes.

Except for an old man in a baseball cap, the group stood in glum silence, staring off into space. The old man, who stood closest to the door, leaned on a cane and cheerfully carried on a one-way conversation with the young woman standing second in line.

"I gotta come in once a month for labs, you know, and I gotta be fasting. So I always make sure to get here by 7:30, so I can get in first. But even when I get here at 7:30," he gestured with his free hand over his shoulder at the door behind him, "they never seem to get my blood drawn before 8:30."

At this, the young woman responded. "Why does it take so long? At this rate, I'll be late for my new job!" She sounded dismayed and looked impatiently at her watch.

"Well, I don't wanna badmouth nobody or nothing." The man adjusted the cap on his head. "But this place is really bad. I used to go to the lab over on Solano. Boy was that place great. You know there was only this one guy working over there and he could of processed all these people in a snap. Wouldn't you know it, but just my luck and my insurance changed. Now I've gotta come here. But I'm telling you, these guys... You should check your insurance and see if you can go to that other lab."

When I heard this, I gritted my teeth in frustration. I already knew my insurance limited me to this particular lab. I should have realized it would be bad when I saw the sign on the building announcing that the lab was affiliated with the hospital of my hemodialysis horror and early PD troubles. I turned to Bob.

"If what he says is true, they're probably not going to get to me for another hour. But that could really screw up the results. You know I'm fasting, right? The whole point of these labs is to measure my cyclosporine level and make sure it doesn't fall off too much. If it does, I could have a rejection episode."

I felt my tension level rise. I hated waiting, and I'm sure the sixty-milligrams of prednisone I was currently taking wasn't helping. It made me sweat and vibrate with an excitable, nervous energy.

Bob looked up from his newspaper. "Why don't you take the cyclosporine later on Wednesday night?" (I had to come back for labs twice a week for the next month and would be back here again on Thursday morning.) "Wouldn't that work?" he asked.

"No, you don't understand."

When the social worker had reviewed my medications in the hospital, she'd warned me that cyclosporine was hard on the stomach and that I would need time to digest it before lying down to sleep, or else I risked damaging my stomach lining. She had also told me to take the prescribed anti-ulcer drug just before bedtime as an extra protection for my stomach.

Bob nodded as he listened to me explain, but then he patted my hand and murmured, "Don't fret. You'll get your labs drawn. Just be patient, my dear."

His platitude didn't help. By the time the lab assistant finally opened the door at 8:10 a.m., I was almost in tears. I hurried to the front desk, past the other waiting people to explain my situation.

"You have got to draw my blood now." I leaned forward across the desk, urgent and wildly dramatic. "I just had a kidney transplant last week and I took my last dose of cyclosporine at 8 p.m. last night—over twelve hours ago! The doctors told me I have to take the cyclosporine every twelve hours exactly, or I risk a rejection episode! You have got to understand: my husband gave me my new kidney and I am not going to risk losing it!"

My urgency worked this first time and the lab assistant bumped me up to second in line. Nevertheless, I realized that in order to comply with my medication regimen, I would have to come and wait at least as early as 7:30 a.m., if I wanted to make sure I would be seen as close to 8 a.m. as possible.

A Second Chance

By the Thursday after my labs, I managed to sit up long enough to face the three hundred plus emails that had built up in my inbox. By the following Monday, Kurt was back to work in person and I began telecommuting. Fortunately, because we lived in Berkeley, Kurt commuted to work by carpool or BART and didn't have to drive himself into the City.

Monday afternoon, Cara put me on a call with ITWear's new PR firm. Before connecting them on the three-way system, she alerted me.

"Hey, Lisa-Lisa. The agency doesn't know you're at home right now. I told them you've been away on vacation the last two weeks. Hey, it just occurred to me, I can't call you 'Kidneyless Wonder' anymore!"

"Yep, no more dialysis disco," I laughed.

Our new PR agency hadn't known about my health situation, and the teleconference proceeded as though everything was completely normal.

When I hung up, I didn't immediately return to editing the press release I'd been working on before the call. Instead,

I stared blankly at the laptop screen and thought about my life now.

On the one hand, it felt strange that nothing had changed, at least in relation to my job, and yet everything was really so incredibly different. I remembered when I came home from the hospital and looked into the mirror for the first time after the transplant, gone were the yellow eyes and skin. Now the whites of my eyes shown bright and my skin radiated pink health.

I took a bite of the decadent brownie on the plate beside my laptop and reveled in guilt-free delight. I could eat chocolate now without worrying about surging phosphorus levels. I could eat dinner with Kurt again, too. No longer did I have to rush home and eat as soon as possible in order to hook up to the dialysis machine by 8 p.m., and I was finally free of the renal-friendly diet and its emphasis on animal protein.

I celebrated my new freedom Monday night by making one of my old favorites, pasta with vegetarian marinara and a green salad.

"How was your first day back in the office?" I asked Kurt over dinner.

"Good. I was a little tired, but it was great seeing everyone again and getting so much attention. Jim Kense even came by my office and welcomed me back!" Kurt straightened in his chair, proud.

"Wow, a visit from the CEO! You are well loved. And boy have you earned a lot of karma points," I teased, taking a sip of grape juice, or "faux wine" as I called it. Real wine still gave me heartburn.

"But seriously," I continued, "I'm glad you've healed so well. It's hard to believe that not even two weeks ago you had surgery. They took a kidney out of you, but you're still completely fine. Your kidney is in me now, right here." I patted the left side of my abdomen. "It's doing everything, can you believe it? I don't need dialysis anymore, thanks to your kidney." I wiped away tears. "You've given me a second chance at life. I don't know how I can thank you. I love you."

"I love you, too."

He reached across the table and took my hands in his. After a moment, he pulled back and lightened the tone.

"You know that this means you owe me for life, right? So, whenever I need anything, you have to give it to me," he grinned.

"Of course," I laughed.

That night, I slipped freely into bed. It would be another week before the bandages came off my scar, but, as I pulled the covers up and moved over to snuggle Kurt, I celebrated the freedom to roll about the bed without having to worry about pinching the catheter and tubing. No alarms or machine noises would disturb my sleep tonight.

Before drifting off, I reflected on the year that had passed. What a year! After all I'd endured on dialysis, I'd come to think of myself as someone quite different from the Lisa I'd been before kidney failure. I'd grown to accept this new identity over the last year. But with the second chance Kurt's kidney offered, everything had changed again. Who was I now?

Chapter 12 - Denouement

In the months following the transplant, I reveled in the freedom Kurt's kidney gave me. Now I could slip easily between the sheets to sleep, unencumbered by tubing or machinery. Showering and swimming no longer involved special precautions or fears of infection. I no longer had to take supplements to keep my calcium level low whenever I ate anything. My body once again made its own red blood cells, so I no longer had to give myself the thrice-weekly Epogen shots. Every time I went to the bathroom, I marveled that Kurt's kidney gave me the power to pee and that it diligently worked around the clock to purge my body of toxins and regulate my chemistry. His kidney even gave me back my femininity—in less than two months after the transplant, I began menstruating again.

Perhaps most miraculous of all is that Kurt has suffered no ill effects of having donated his kidney to me. One kidney was powerful enough to restore me to health and one kidney has been enough for Kurt to maintain his quality of life. In the summer that followed the transplant, we backpacked Cherry Creek again, and the summer after that, we explored the fantastic, high elevation, almost extraterrestrial Eastern Sierra realm of Evolution Basin.

Kurt still climbs mountains, rides bikes, and performs spectacular feats of physical prowess. His lab values are all within normal limits and his blood pressure remains low. That nature designed us to have two kidneys and that it is possible to remove one, put it in another person's body, and then have each kidney almost double in size to take over dual functioning, is miraculous. Despite missing a kidney, Kurt is as healthy as ever.

Unlike Kurt, I haven't returned completely to my original health. Cyclosporine and prednisone, two of the immunosuppressants I have to take for the rest of my life, trigger high blood pressure, so I have to take blood pressure medicine. Azathioprine, the other immunosuppressant, puts me at risk for skin cancer. I wear hats, sunscreen, and avoid being outside between 10 a.m. and 4 p.m., but I continue to have occasional incidents of squamous cell carcinomas. I make sure to see the dermatologist twice a year and check my skin regularly.

I also still have labs drawn periodically in order to check my cyclosporine level and check that the kidney is OK, which entails the hassle of fasting and traveling to the local lab first thing in the morning. Within months of the transplant, my labs revealed that my cholesterol had climbed too high, another unfortunate side effect of cyclosporine. Like many Americans, I take a statin and watch my cholesterol intake, made even more important when I learned that high cholesterol can adversely affect the kidney as well as the heart.

Despite the triple punch of the immunosuppressive drugs, I've been fortunate not to have suffered any serious illness as a result of immunosuppression, except for occasional urinary tract infections. I try to practice good hygiene and avoid exposing myself to germs. And I make sure to take my medication.

On dialysis, I'd grown used to a life at one-tenth my previous capacity. Without all the wild energy and hormones coursing through me, combined with the meditation practice, I had enjoyed a profound sensation of calm, something that I'd never before experienced. Everything changed yet again with the transplant. The high dose of prednisone I was initially prescribed inflamed the enormous surge of health that was re-transforming me. Unlike Gabrielle at the hemodialysis clinic who'd ballooned on prednisone, I didn't gain weight. Instead, I was sweating and euphoric, my mind and body humming, vibrating, almost trembling with the intensity of good feeling. Meditation became that much more difficult, and gone was the amazing ability to focus, to see clearly the path ahead.

The Crash

While my personal life improved after the transplant, the world around me fell apart. In March 2000, the month of the transplant, the stock market reached its zenith, but by April, it started to slide. ITWear didn't escape the downward trend. Though the dotcom boom flourished for more than three years and created an era of boundless financial optimism and a culture that worshipped youth, innovation, and all things newer, better, faster, more efficient, the era came to an end almost as quickly as it began.

ITWear's stock crested at $99/share in March 2000, but like the rest of the tech sector, it then began to fall. Our CEO, struggled to maintain his optimistic outlook against each month's precipitous drop, but as the months moved on and the price plummeted irreversibly downward, a dark negativity spread among the ITWearians and infected all of us with the premonition of impending disaster.

When things had gone well, my job as PR Manager had been fun, arranging press interviews for Percy to talk about ITWear's stellar performance, at least as represented by its stock valuation. Now, if the media was interested in ITWear at all, it was only to talk about how the company's stock was tanking. My job was reduced to running damage control and attempting to mollify Percy by churning out peppy little press releases, devoid of real news, but which he felt might help pump the stock or at least satisfy the institutional investors that had ITWear by the throat.

Though I felt better physically than I had in almost two years, my job was emotionally dragging me down. By autumn, it felt like things were coming to a head. In November, ITWear's stock slipped below two dollars a share. I'd planned to quit in January, but the decision was made for me in December. Cara had warned me that layoffs were in the works as our CFO crunched the company's numbers for the fall quarterly earnings statement, but her warning didn't prepare me for what came next.

First thing Monday morning, December 1st, 2000, all ITWear employees were called into the main meeting room, or designated rooms at the company's remote locations. A quiet pall descended on the audience when we noticed the burly strangers in bulging suit coats standing at the front and back of the room. Percy came in, his eyes downcast, and began the company meeting. Gone was the cheerful, ebullient knight in shining armor leading his company to victory. In his place sat a tired, middle-aged man, his eyes full of tears and his voice cracking, as he proceeded to lay off fifty percent of the company.

At the time, I was happy to receive the severance package, which I wouldn't have received if I'd voluntarily quit in January. But the layoffs at ITWear weren't an isolated event. All around us, the dotcom boom and the economy it had produced in the Bay Area collapsed. Public relations and marketing were fields particularly devastated.

In the months that followed, I learned that Helen's agency had been acquired and her staff let go. She herself was pregnant with twins. Only one of her seven employees remained in PR. Two moved out of state, another became a real estate agent. Kristen, who I'd admired as a paragon of equilibrium, one of the most well-adjusted, "normal" people I'd known, was now a harried mom, struggling to deal with an unusually difficult child, her hair messy, her clothes dirty, and pregnant with her second baby.

Within six months of the December layoffs, ITWear laid off another round and eliminated its marketing department completely, and this time Cara lost her job. Perhaps most telling was when Kurt and I learned that our friend Patrick, who'd first inspired us to move to the Bay Area when his company was bought and he retired, now had to return to work, his stock portfolio decimated by the stock market crash. The Internet boom was a bust. The events of September 11, less than a year later, destroyed whatever optimism might have been left and unequivocally marked the end of an era.

The Future

The transplant has enabled me to regain much of what I had before kidney failure, but I am not the same person I used to be. My dead kidneys, my time on dialysis, and my life as a transplant recipient have permanently colored my identity. My relationship with the medical establishment is now a given, especially when I consider that Kurt's kidney may not last the rest of my life. With time, the weightiness of these issues has slowly lessened as I've sought to integrate my past with my present and potential futures.

Time has had an ameliorating effect. New memories overwrite older ones. The approach of Winter Solstice no longer reminds me solely of that infamous Fall, when my kidneys were slowly dying and I descended into darkness. It's been distanced by subsequent autumns, new events, and my current health status. With each passing year, what had been a horrible loss and devastation becomes more easily a memory, a part of me, but something no longer dominating the present moment.

I haven't conquered my fear. In the dark times, when I worry that the anti-GBM disease might return and attack Kurt's kidney or that some other disease might attack, something more invasive and less self-limiting than anti-GBM disease, I remind myself that I have been there, in that sick space, before. I have been to hell and back. Remembering this helps me believe that if I have to, I can go there again, and I will survive. This process of remembering may not necessarily cheer me up, but it does give me courage. I can face what might happen and, more importantly, these thoughts remind me not to take the present moment for granted. Right here, right now, I feel OK—and that is, in itself, a miracle.

THE END

###

Afterword

We are all ships afloat on the sea of time, the current flows and bears us forward into the future, forever altering how we make sense of our pasts.

I wrote this memoir in the first two years after my transplant, but it hasn't been until now, fourteen years later, that I'm ready to send it out into the world for you to read. Though I have cleaned up some of the awkward writing and tightened up a few of the scenes, it still stands as something I wrote in the immediate aftermath of my experience on dialysis.

You should know that if I were to write the memoir today, it would reflect a different consciousness, a different geography in the course of my life history. It would be a happier book, replete with the exciting and wonderful experiences that have influenced the healthy, middle-aged person that I have become. Most of all, it would include the birth of my daughter, Lila, born four and a half years after the transplant. She is healthy and thriving, a living testimony to the power of modern medicine.

Acknowledgements

I would like to thank first and foremost, my husband Kurt. The magic his kidney performs inside me every day is a gift beyond words. I am deeply grateful for the support of my parents, Elsa and Bob, and my sister Marla. They have always been there for me and I know they always will. Thanks, Bob, for taking the lovely photo of Kurt and me all those years ago that now graces the cover of this book.

I am also indebted to Holly McArthur, Carole Sinclair and all the other women who made up the Capstone team, as well as Peter Jackson and the folks at Intraware. They stood by me during my year on dialysis and gave me a reason to get up in the morning.

Terry Healey's helpful advice about the publishing business inspired me to make this memoir a published reality. Rebecca Douglass and Emily Cooke helped me revise early versions of this manuscript and offered valuable emotional support through the writing process. Hillary Avis, Elizabeth Fergason, Jenness Hobart, Staci Homrig, and Deborah Romani provided important feedback on the final project.

Thanks to the incredible doctors and nurses at California Pacific Medical Center (CPMC), in particular Dr. Steven Katznelson and Chris Becker, whose dedicated and conscientious care have made all the difference. And finally, I would like to thank David Weinberg, who taught me how to breathe.

About the Author

Lisa Frieden grew up in Southern California and earned degrees in English and American Literature and Languages from Harvard University and UC Santa Barbara. She has worked in high tech public relations, survived a year on dialysis, underwent a kidney transplant, and is now a wife, a mother, and a writer. She is the author of the romantic suspense novel, *The Offering*. She currently resides in the San Francisco Bay Area and is at work on her next novel. www.lisafrieden.com.

Other Books by Lisa Frieden

The Offering

Finding Clarity in the Emerald Triangle: a romantic thriller (with echoes of Deliverance) - COMING SOON

DIALYSIS: A MEMOIR

www.ingramcontent.com/pod-product-compliance
Lightning Source LLC
Chambersburg PA
CBHW020613300426
44113CB00007B/630